HOW TO GET A GIRLFRIEND
Two Classic Dating Guides in One Volume

Understanding Women
and
How To Be The Man Women Want

HOW TO GET A GIRLFRIEND
Two Classic Dating Guides in One Volume

Understanding Women
and
How To Be The Man Women Want

ROMY MILLER

LEISURE CREST INTERNATIONAL

For RKR

This edition published in 2009 by Leisure Crest International.

Understanding Women copyright © 2004 by Romy Miller
How To Be The Man Women Want copyright © 2009 by Romy Miller

Paperback ISBN-13: 978-1-932420-88-3
Paperback ISBN-10: 1-932420-88-6

First published by New Tradition Books in 2004 and 2009.

Published by Leisure Crest International.

eBook ISBN–13: 978-1-932420-89-0
eBook ISBN–10: 1-932420-89-4

Disclaimer: This book is not intended to replace medical advice or be a substitute for a psychologist. The author and the publisher expressly disclaim responsibility for any adverse affects of this book. Neither author nor publisher is liable for information contained herein.

.

Author's note:

THIS ISN'T A PICKUP GUIDE

In recent years, there has been a deluge of pickup guides to hit the market. While this is all well and good, it seems that these guides have hindered men more than they've helped them. I've heard of embarrassments suffered from using the techniques in these books. I've also heard of men just having no luck in general.

This isn't a pickup guide. The two books contained in this volume are guides on how to meet and date women. They aren't about playing games or tricks in order to get laid. These books are about finding fulfillment with the opposite sex. They are about finding that special girl with whom to have a relationship. Or how to have fun dating until you find her.

If this is something you want, you have come to the right place and I hope I can help you with that. But you have to know that if you want to meet someone, it is up to you to get it in gear and get out there. It's not all about looks or money or what kind of car you drive. But it is about the kind of person you are. And just being yourself and being secure in your own skin is what we're after. It's not about presenting an image to a woman and hoping she'll latch on. It's about finding someone who likes you for you. And, hopefully, by the end of this book, you'll be on your way.

The best advice I can give you on your journey is to simply, relax. And to use your sense of humor. If you can learn to laugh at the dating situation you find yourself in—and stop taking it so seriously—you're going to automatically free yourself up for better women. And, you have to know, all women love a guy with a great sense of humor.

One last note. If you are a person who gets easily offended, this might not be the book for you. It is one hard truth after another. I don't pull any punches. However, if you can chill a little and just listen to what I have to say, it will help you. But you have to be willing to be open to the ideas contained in this book. And, usually, being open to new ideas is all it takes to make a change. So, if you're ready to make a change, then let's get to it. Time is a'wastin'.

UNDERSTANDING WOMEN
The Definitive Guide to Meeting, Dating and
Dumping, if Necessary

CONTENTS

MY MISSION: TO TURN YOU INTO A DATING MACHINE

Let's face facts. You probably don't know that much about women. Don't be upset. You know it's true. You need help, don't you? This isn't going to be easy but it's time, isn't it? Yeah, you know it is.

You've tried to meet someone but haven't had a date in a long time. You can't even remember the last time you *spoke* with a woman. In fact, the last woman you saw naked was on the internet.

I feel your pain, buddy, I really, really do.

And you've done everything in your power to hook up—from internet dating services to dating books. None of it helped. Mostly because you rarely get what you see on a computer—from a sweater to a woman it never looks quite the same. And those books were mostly written by men. Most men don't really have a clue as to what women really want or even what they're all about. That's because men's perception of women is an entirely different thing than how women actually are. They're just as confused as you are! Some might have a smidgen of good advice but if I wanted advice about women, I would go to the source—a woman.

It's not your fault that you're just a normal guy. You have a normal job and lead a normal life. Or maybe you're one of those internet millionaires and still can't seem to get a date. Regardless of your social status, there's help for you unless you have a tail and horns. (If you do, my apologies.)

Perhaps you've had a lot of dates but nothing seems to come out of them. You might be to the point where you've given up on it all. You've thrown in the towel and told yourself that women, simply, aren't worth it. You've been rejected and scorned and hey, maybe someone *threw* something at you. But you're not a bad guy, are you? No. You just can't figure chicks out. What do they want? Why do they behave in the manner they do? Why are they so elusive? And why do I still want them when they don't seem to want me?

I'm gonna help you with all that.

Let's talk about why you feel the way you do. I mean, not the rejected part, but the part that still wants women. Simply put, you have a biological imperative to mate. It's ingrained in you to go after a chick that you find attractive, mate with her and have a baby. *Whoa!*—you say—*nobody said anything about babies!* Listen, Einstein, that's why you want it. Sure, it's fun but the bottom line is you want to get your rocks off and the reason you want to is because you want to spread your genes. Getting a baby may not be what you want, but it's definitely what your hormones are screaming for. It's called "biology."

I told you this wasn't going to be easy.

That's why these feelings never go away and torture you on an every day—if not every hour—basis. You can't run away from it; you will never escape it. You need women like women need new shoes.

Heavy, huh? No, it doesn't have to be.

So, if it's all "biological," why are chicks so hard to figure out? Since the advent of the Independent Woman, it seems as though men have been left by the way-side. Women don't have to be as interested as they used to be. She can hire a handy-man to fix that leaky faucet and she can go to a sperm bank for a baby and she can buy a vibrator to please herself. So why does she need to expend the effort to meet you?

Again, it's all biological.

She *does* want you. She *does* need you. She's just gotten a little pickier and a little more ornery over the past few decades. However, we, as humans, are wired to want each other and not battery operated devices that give mind-blowing, though albeit, short orgasms. We have to have each other. We crave each other. Without each other…well, why bother with any of it?

That's where I come in.

So why did *I* write a book like this anyway? What makes *me* such an expert on this tantalizing subject? After all, I could make a lot more money doing internet porn. Well, think about it. Men don't understand women. I don't care how many degrees they have, they don't get it. I am a woman so it should stand to reason I know a little about what women want and how they tick. Additionally, I've also dated a few men in my time and you can learn from *their* mistakes.

If you are willing to listen to me, I am going to tell you how women tick. And what makes them tick and why they tick. I will dispel the rumors, the half-truths. I will turn you into a dating machine and you will have your pick of any beautiful woman you want. You'll wonder why you didn't try this sooner.

Not only that, I'm going to tell you what to do *after* you get that date. I am going to tell you how to keep her—that is, if you want to keep her—after it's all said and done and some practical advice on sex. With this information at your disposal, it won't take long to get what you want and deserve.

Most chapters are going to be short and to the point, mostly because it shouldn't take a gazillion years to explain something as simple as women and their womanly wiles. As you read this stuff, you might say to yourself, *"A lot of this is just common sense."* Apparently, no, it isn't. And using the term common sense only seems to add to the confusion. If it were all common sense, then everyone would already know everything. And that's not the case. If you follow my advice in this book, you will be what is commonly known as a "Catch." Even if your relationships have never worked out before, take some of my advice, if not all, and the word will get around about you and how great you are.

Hopefully, after you read this, you are going to be so cool that women are going to be asking *you* out. Know how to treat her right and the rest will follow. The more you know, the better you can understand the dynamics of that wonderful creature we call *Woman.*

THE BASIC RULES OF DATING WOMEN

You will notice that there appears to be a lot of double standards in the dating world. Like, why are guys always expected to pay for dinner? (I still don't understand why men get so hung up on this.) Yes, there are a lot of double standards but so what? You wanna get lucky or not? If so, learn that just because something's a double standard doesn't mean you can change it for all mankind by simply refusing to give into it. You need to know that there are plenty of smart men out there who don't let little things like this get in the way of dating and/or getting lucky.

If you have the attitude that you don't have to "work for it," and that you should be able to date a woman simply based on the merit that you have a penis, then take a moment and look around. You're not the only guy on the planet, are you? There are a lot of other guys out there who also have penises. Now, take a moment and think about what distinguishes you from all these other men. What makes you so special? It might be your knowledge that you are willing to work for it. You aren't like these other guys who think women should just fall at your feet. You know that's not going to happen to any other man, unless, of course, he's a rock star and even rock stars are in short supply these days.

In essence, you are a man who knows that being the guy women want also entails giving them *what* they want. *That* makes you special. What also make you special is that you're not a jerk. Women hate jerks. They dislike men who treat them like crap. But if you distinguish yourself from all these jerks, then you will come out on top. Sure, it may take some time, but it will happen. Women like good guys. Becoming a good guy is all it takes to land a wonderful woman.

There may still be something bothering you. What does make you so special? How do you let a woman know you're worth it? If these are your questions, I believe that an old nemesis, insecurity, has raised its ugly little head. You may have a million excuses but when you look at them close enough, maybe they all add up to the fact that you're afraid you'll expend the effort and get nothing in return. Will this happen? Who knows? But know that if you never try, you can never hope to get what you want.

SOME EXCUSES:
- I don't have any money.
- I don't have enough confidence.
- Women don't like me.
- I don't have the looks.

These are just excuses for you not to get up and do something. That's all. If you're looking for an excuse, you *will* find it. Ask yourself if you really and truly want to spend the rest of your life alone. If you do, fine. Say hello to your comic book collection for me. If not, let's get to work.

But before we go any further, I am going to concentrate this chapter on the basics of women and of dating. This isn't every single thing included in the book. It's just a basic overview that should give you a general idea of what's going on.

THE BASIC RULES OF WOMEN:

- Each and every one of them is unique. Once you figure one of them out, another will throw you a curve ball. There's nothing you can do about it, either.
- Not all women are unapproachable and that includes very beautiful women. Sometimes, very beautiful women aren't approached *because* of their beauty. Many men are afraid of rejection and don't approach them. So they appreciate what little attention they get.
- Women love to talk and they especially love to talk about themselves. If you can get her to talk about herself, all you have to do is nod occasionally and pay attention to what she's saying. (Or, at the very least, pretend to pay attention.)
- No woman likes to be perceived as easy, even if she is.
- Women love gifts and that includes jewelry.
- Women are picky about everything. Why wouldn't she be picky about who she dates? You have to make it worth her time.
- Women like to date men who are worth it to her. If you're a "fixer-upper" with bad clothes, body and teeth, she's not going to expend the effort. Unless, of course, you've just won the lottery.
- Women love to be seduced, romanced and pampered.
- Women are in control. This is the biggest thing you will ever learn. In dating, women are totally in control. You, obviously, plan the date, but she calls the shots and it's her decision if you have sex or not.
- On the flip side of this, women want a man who takes control in the bedroom. If you can rock her world, you'll never get rid of her.

THE BASIC RULES OF DATING:

- While you do not have to be extraordinary good looking or rich you do need to be: Clean, in good, physical shape, sharply dressed and smell nice.
- Never brag or lie. It's always best to present an honest image. If you start to date a woman, she's going to find out about you eventually anyway.
- There are three types of men: the Confident Man, the Bad Boy and the Smart Guy. Learn to combine elements from all three of these types and you should have women falling all over you.
- Never allow a woman to pay for anything, even if she insists.
- Clothes do matter.
- Good grooming matters, too.
- Never invite yourself over to a chick's apartment. She will assume *you* assume she's a slut. No woman wants to be perceived as easy. (See basic rules of women.)
- It is up to you to date. If you don't take the initiative, then nothing will ever happen. Women will not come to you. You have to go to them.
- Never insult a woman.
- Never try to get a woman in bed.
- Never hit a woman.
- Never disrespect a woman even if she does it to you. Just take it like a man and she'll be the one who looks bad.
- Never think that you deserve to get laid just because you paid for dinner.
- The main thing you need is confidence. Confidence to dress nice. Confidence to approach women. Confidence to get rejected without it killing you. Confidence, confidence, confidence!

READY, SET, GO!

I know you're ready to hit the streets and turn yourself into a dating machine, but first things first. You need to mentally prepare yourself for your new adventures in dating. And by this I mean, get yourself physically and mentally ready.

Let me say one more thing. I know there are a lot of whiners out there who will whimper when they realize they're not perfect. They'll also cry when they realize that they are going to have to improve on themselves so they can get date. Improving yourself by buying new clothes or getting rid of your beer belly doesn't have to kill you. In fact, it's only going to help you.

An important thing to keep in mind is that not *every* chick you run across is going to dig you. There are some chicks out there who really don't like anyone for whatever reason. That's life. All you have to do is weed those chicks out. Don't beat yourself up if you get rejected a few times. Expect it and then when you finally get some acceptance, it will be all the sweeter.

Always remember that while this may be a lot to consume, it is the winners who do stuff that losers don't want to do. Winners will take chances and search for opportunity. If you're not willing to get up off the couch and improve on yourself, you haven't got a chance in scoring.

One of the most important things to do before you try to pick up a girl is to go out and observe them. Sounds stupid, but be a girl watcher. Watch how she acts and what she does. Watch couples together. Watch other guys trying to pick up chicks. Learn from their mistakes. Watch, listen, observe. Take time to do this. It's important to know what you're up against. (Also, don't be too obvious when you do this. You don't want to give the "voyeur" vibe off.)

WHAT WE LEARNED:
- You have to improve on yourself.
- Not all women are going to dig you, just like you don't dig all women.
- Don't be afraid of rejection. I know it can hurt, but if you never try, you never give anyone an opportunity to say yes.

BUT I JUST WANT TO GET LAID!

Maybe all you want is some poontang. You lament, *All I want to do is get laid. Tell me how to get laid for God's sake! I don't care about all this other stuff!* It's all about the sex to you, isn't it? If so, go hire an escort. It's really pretty simple, if that's all you want.

Do you really want to be one of those guys who use women just for sex? Let me tell you, the word will get out pretty quickly on your bad habits. Girls talk and if the word gets out, you're going to be in even worse condition than when you started. Also, by doing this, you put yourself at risk for all kinds of diseases. Any skank will have sex with you if you get her drunk enough. But if you want a good/real woman who doesn't necessarily have to get liquored up to have sex with you, you are going to have to put in some effort. Like it or lump it. If you want to find someone and, as Desmond Morris says, form a pair bond, then you are going to have to work a little.

Of course you're saying, *but I don't care about the pair bond* and if you are, shame on you! You just need to sit, back, relax and open your eyes. By the time I am finished, getting laid will be the least of your worries. If you're still not convinced, go on. Put the book down and try it *your* way. Let me know how it works out.

Let me outline a few facts for you. Getting laid is great and it feels wonderful. Believe me, I know. But if all you ever do is hop from one bed to another and never form any sort of relationship, you're going to end up alone. Think about your uncle. The one who's alone and drinks a lot. The one who smells funny and tells dirty jokes no one gets. Is this what you want? Do you want to end up like your uncle? No, you don't. And you don't have to! However, if you don't work on this stuff—yourself mainly—then it won't matter how many women you have sex with, you always feel alienated from them. Besides, how can you expect to have sex with women if you don't understand how they operate?

Women are your friends; they're your buddies. You've just got to learn about them and learn how to work them. There are no real dating techniques. What works for one won't work for another. There are some universal truths, however, and that's what we're going to concentrate on. Once you're ready to face up to the truth, then and only then can you be ready to go out and pursue the woman of your dreams, whoever she may be. Once you know what you're dealing with, you can approach any woman out there with confidence. And if you get her in bed and then want to leave her, that's your business. All I can say is if that's what you're after, then you've got some real intimacy issues to work on. And that's your problem.

Chances are if you're reading this book, you're lonely and don't have that someone special in your life. Am I right? You want to take that step in the right direction and get your life moving. You do want a family on down the line but nothing seems to be working right now. No matter how hard you try, something isn't clicking.

Or, are you trying too hard? Maybe. Maybe you're not really trying at all. But I can tell you this, the more effort you put into getting dates and forming pair bonds, the more you will get out. If you do this, you will have a person you can share stuff with. You will always have a date on Saturday nights. And isn't that much better than going to Ladies' Night?

I think so.

You also need to realize that women are just as confused about men as you are them. For the most part, none of us have you figured out. We want to know what makes you tick as much as you want to know what makes us tick. We're all so fascinated with each other. But that doesn't keep us from playing mind games does it?

Nope. And then it all gets tangled and messy and weird. How can we hook up with each other with as little pain as possible? How the hell can a man approach a woman without worrying about getting his head bitten off?

I think one of the main problems in the dating world is that we tend to over-intellectualize everything. We overanalyze and try to second guess everyone's next move. We don't give people enough time to react or, for that matter, to size us up before we're all over them, trying to impress them. Then we're kicking ourselves for even talking to them. Hooking up should not be as hard as it is, but for some reason, it is.

Because we tend to over-intellectualize everything, everything gets skewed and that makes everyone a bit crazy. That's why it's so hard to walk up to a chick and ask her out on a date. What if she says no? How about this? *What if she says yes?*

After I'm done with you, she might.

Don't believe me? Then that tells me you are one of the walking wounded. Do not be one of the walking wounded. If you think that chicks will reject you before you even ask them out, they probably will. It's all in your attitude. If you look and feel good about yourself, then other people will see that too. You can't feel sorry for yourself anymore. It hasn't worked in the past, has it? You need to learn to shrug off rejection. It will smart for a while but the more comfortable you become with yourself, the better off you will be. And the easier everything will get.

Know this: There is no instant gratification. Unless you're a rock star, you are not going to get laid easily. Stop running away. Stop asking for an easier way. There is no easy way to date. None! You will have to work to get what you want. It's up to you. No one can help you but you. I want this book to be a wake-up call for men who have failed at relationships or who have never even gotten one off the ground. And if all you do want to do is get laid, how about this? How about getting laid with someone who cares about you? Who will enjoy being around you? That's much better than picking up the random ho to party with. Once you find someone special, your life will be special. You will have stuff to look forward to. Places to go. New people to meet and new experiences to have. And it all starts here. Right here. Right now. Today. It starts with you.

I can hear you saying, "Yeah, I'll do this tomorrow." Fine. And tomorrow, you can put it off again. Why not start it today? Right now? This instant. Own up to whatever it is in your past that has gotten you down. Face it like a man and then move on from it. Heal yourself. You don't have to do drugs or go to a psychologist to figure out what's wrong with you. Look inside yourself—and not in a new-agey kinda way—and figure out what's blocking you from living the life you want to. Face your fears of isolation or being unsuccessful or whatever they may be. Once you do that, everything will fall into place.

The old cliché says, "Never put off tomorrow what you can do today." And why should you put it off? There's no real reason. The sooner you get it done, the sooner you can find your beautiful girl.

Okay. Stop rolling your eyes. I'll stop with the psychobabble for now. We have many important things to discuss.

WHAT WE LEARNED:
- If getting laid is all you're after, there are plenty of women out there who get paid for such things.
- We all need someone special in our lives.

- Own up to any problems or blocks you might have. Once you get through them, the world is your oyster.
- There is no instant gratification. Work for what you want and soon enough, you'll get it.

PICKY, PICKY

We all know the old saying, "A woman needs a man like a fish needs a bicycle." Some famous feminist said it and the funny thing is, it's true.

What most every guy wants, if I can be crude, is to get laid. (We covered this in the last chapter.) Women don't necessarily have to have this. Sure, it's real nice, but is it worth the trouble? Is it worth spending money on new clothes and hairdos and perfume? Is it worth waiting for that damn phone to ring? You have to make yourself worth the trouble. You have to realize that when you first meet, she's not only sizing you up, she's sizing your genes up, too. This is done subconsciously, of course, but she's looking at you as a potential sperm donor. Things race through her mind, subconsciously, "Would he make a good father? Are his genes good? Would he be able to take care of me and a baby if necessary?"

Let's face facts. Once you've ejaculated, you're pretty much done. If the woman becomes pregnant after sex, she's got nine months of hell and then eighteen-plus years of hard labor in front of her. Given that, you'd be picky, too.

One thing you are going to have to do before you begin to transform your life is to stop whining about how difficult women are. We've went through a lot of crap to get here and we're not about to just give it up. A woman's role today is *not* of a subordinate. More than anything she is your genetic superior. Think about it. She can pop a baby out of her vagina. You can't.

Keep in mind that women don't hate men. Just so you'll know, it's not true. I'll say it again: *Women don't hate men.* Women hate the men who have hurt them. So before you call her a "Man hating bitch," remember that she's probably been hurt by one of your kind and is still smarting from it. Don't take it personally.

WHAT WE LEARNED:

- Women have the right to be picky.
- All women are not "men hating bitches."
- Try to respect and understand her as much as possible. It's not you who's going to be knocked up, is it?

THREE TYPES OF MEN

Before I say anything else, let me say that I realize that most of you aren't looking for a soul mate. Most of you just want to date a little before finding the right woman. And that's cool. You want a stable of women at your disposal, and, hey, who doesn't? But before you can get your stable, you are going to have to locate this little thing called *confidence*.

A man without confidence is like a martini without an olive. Or nachos without cheese. It just doesn't work. Women want men who have confidence. Women do not want a doormat nor do they want a man they will have to reassure all the time. "Oh, you are too wonderful, honey. Don't worry! I love you!" That's a pain in the butt. Besides, once you're together, it's going to be *you* who has to reassure her most of the time.

I am going to describe the three types of men that women love. As you read, try to take attributes of each of these guys and apply them to yourself. It shouldn't be that hard.

CONFIDENT MAN:

We all know that some guys have all the luck. They get everything they want and don't even have to work for it. They're born rich or handsome or both. God! How unfair! They're either born knowing how to pick-up women or they've learned from their lothario fathers. These guys can be complete jerks and still have women falling all over them.

You might not be one of these guys. But you can be if you only knew how.

One of the main things that some of these so-called Confident Men have is...well, confidence. They have loads of confidence. I know this guy who is not the best looking guy in the world. He's short and skinny but he has confidence. He has to beat the chicks off him. He knows what to say and when to say it. Why? Because he doesn't care how the chick reacts; he's just looking to goad her a little. Women loved to be teased and he knows how to push those buttons.

Here's his secret: He thinks he's the best there is. He knows in his heart that he's good. He has confidence. He doesn't fear rejection and isn't afraid to approach a woman, nor he is afraid to let one "get away" every once in a while. He knows that another one will appear soon enough. He figures if a woman doesn't want him, then it's her loss. The Confident Man doesn't have to be rich or intelligent or handsome. He just has to be confident. And he's confident because he knows he can give women what they all want: A good time. He's a little bit of a mystery and a little bit of a jerk. Not much, but a little just to let her know if she decides to leave him, it won't be long before another one takes her place. This way, he keeps her interested. He knows he's a man and she's a woman and because of that, he never beats around the bush.

He never stares at the woman he's trying to woo the entire time. He looks around, but from time to time, he stares her directly in the eye, allowing a small smile to play on his lips. He also lets his eyes dart to her cleavage every once in a while and he also sips his drink while he's talking. He's always on and for that reason, she's usually turned on by him.

Another way to look at it: He's laid-back. This does not mean he's cocky. He's *always* a gentleman.

Once you learn more about women, you can start pushing their buttons—in a good way. Women love for men to pay attention to them. But there has to be something special about that man who's giving the attention. What is that special something? As I've said before, it's just confidence. That's all it is! This shouldn't be a secret but for some reason, it is. You have to have confidence to walk up to her and to offer to buy her a drink. You have to have confidence as you're talking to her—the "She should be glad I'm taking the time" kind of confidence. And you will have it in time.

IN REVIEW: Learn to be more confident. Learn to be a little flirty once you've got a chick's attention. Learn how to push her buttons in the good way. Learn to let her go if she chooses and never let it bother you if she disses you. So what if it doesn't work out? Move on to the next woman.

THE (ELUSIVE) BAD BOY:

I've never seen the big deal, but a lot of women want the Bad Boy. They think that they will get to see the loving side of this guy, that he will be a teddy bear and that only *they* will crack his tough exterior to see the scared little boy inside that they can shape and mold and, obviously, heal.

And, that my friends, is why women like the bad boy. He's a challenge. In my opinion, he's a pain in the butt. And I say this because most times he's going to be a jerk. Women may get their bad boys but they also get a lot of pain to go along with him. And usually, they get a cheater to go along with their pain. The funny thing about this is, if they are successful in reforming the Bad Boy, they usually find that they don't want him anymore. He's no longer interesting.

You don't have to be a bad boy to get women. The thing that bad boys do that rest of you don't is that they hold back. They don't fawn over women. They'll give a girl a good once-over, then stare her directly in the eye. This makes her see that he's aggressive enough to do something but for some reason he's holding back. Then her little mind goes to racing. *Why isn't he coming to me? Why isn't he doing anything? Don't I look hot tonight?* They don't realize that because he's a Bad Boy, they've got to go to him. Bad Boys don't chase women. Women chase Bad Boys.

Learn that lesson from the Bad Boys. Just hold back. Unless she's a bitch, she will come to you. The great thing is, even if she is a bitch, she'll come on over anyway. *Why is this dude checking me out and not doing anything about it?* Believe me, she wants to know why.

Of course, if you don't have a bunch of tattoos and a Harley parked outside, what are you going to do if she comes over? What are you going to give her? A free drink? Women are attracted to Bad Boys because they think there's something else *there.* Who knows what it may be, but that's why they get so riled up. Of course, realistically, women are attracted to bad boys because they know they are going to take them on a wild ride of some kind— preferably in bed. But once the ride's over, there's a lot of pain to sort through.

You can be a Bad Boy without being bad. All you have to do is take what bad boys do—treat women like meat—and tweak it. You can give them those looks without seeming sleazy. You can be bad in bed but a total gentleman otherwise.

IN REVIEW: Bad Boys act like they have something on women. They are elusive. Act like that and you've got her.

THE SMART GUY:
You want to be one of these guys. Here's what they do:

- Smart guys watch dating shows and pay attention to their friends' dating stories. Let the other guy make the mistake and you learn the lesson. (Figuring out what not to do is just as important as figuring out what to do.)
- Smart guys know when to pull back.
- Smart guys let the chicks know that he notices them and then he makes them wait a little while before he approaches them.
- Smart guys watch shows on human behavior on the Discovery Channel and find out how humans tick.
- Smart guys watch James Bond films and learn a thing or two about the art of seduction and tease from the master.
- Smart guys take mental notes and study women with diligence.
- Smart guys put forth the effort and know if they do, they can get something back.
- Smart guys dress nice, smell nice and are always courteous to a woman even if she disses him. Smoothness is a must.

So, take elements from all three of these men. Take the confidence from the Confident Man, combine it with the elusive nature of the Bad Boy and study it like a Smart Guy. By combining these factors, you will find your own personal pattern and comfort level and then work it. If you can do this, then you won't have to worry. You won't need loads of money or looks. You can be you but with more confidence and know-how. You can be Mr. Normal Guy who's a little bit of a mystery and a touch of the bad boy every girl desires.

But the biggest thing is to have confidence. Once you know you can ask a chick out without falling all over yourself, and that she should be happy you are, you'll have no problem.

There you have it. *That's* the big secret these guys have. You just have to learn to use it to *your* advantage. But, alas, that skill will come in time.

WHAT WE LEARNED:
- There are three types of men: The Confident Man, the Bad Boy and the Smart Guy.
- Combine elements of all three and become a master at seduction and tease.

MYTHS

There are a lot of myths floating around out there about this and about that. Let's go through a few of them, shall we?

MYTH: *You can make anyone fall in love with you.*
TRUTH: This is absolute bull. Of course, after they've known you for a while, sure, maybe. But if you and she don't have the right chemistry, no amount of anything is going to make her fall for you. Do you know that smell has a lot to do with people falling in love? We cover ourselves up with colognes and perfumes so our natural pheromones can't shine through. My advice? Take a good bath, wash everything and use just a touch of cologne. See if it works.

MYTH: *With the right moves, you can get laid by any girl.*
TRUTH: Again, absolute bull. You may be one helluva guy, but not every woman in the whole world is going to want to have sex with you. I don't care if you were her shoulder to cry on or shelter from the storm. I don't care how much you spent on her. She will either like you enough to let you get into her pants or she won't. And, even if you do get lucky, she could still diss you after it's all said and done. Love's a bitch, ain't it?

MYTH: *Learning body language secrets will let you know if a girl likes you.*

TRUTH: Yeah, but what if you're in a dark club? If a girl likes you—really likes you—she isn't going to let you get away if—*if*—you give her a signal that you're interested. The best way to see if a chick likes you is to approach *her*. Women are just as confused and just as nervous about approaching you as you are them. They're looking for signs, too. And what if both of you misread the signs? Well, you're both out of luck, aren't you? If she isn't interested, then it's over and you can move onto the next one.

MYTH: *You have to be rich to get girls nowadays.*
TRUTH: Women like money but guys with money are usually jerks. Sure, they might let them buy them stuff, but will they fall in love with someone who treats them like dirt? Probably not. Besides, do you really want to have to buy her love?

MYTH: *Girls play hard to get.*
TRUTH: This one is true and it's probably one of the stupider things girls do. It's very frustrating to guys. However, it's not going to stop, so you need to learn how to deal with it. One of the reasons girls do this is that they believe that you, the male, are the natural born aggressor. Think about our hunting and gathering days. Women gathered, men hunted. Men were out all day killing wild animals and bringing the chow into camp. If men didn't do it back then, they might not have to do it now. But, alas, you did, so you have to.

It's not going to change. No matter what, women want men who will confidently approach them. Women don't like to chase men. It makes them feel desperate. This does not mean that you have to hound a chick. This means that you should approach her and start talking. Nature should take its course after that initial meeting.

The point is, some of this stuff is true, on a very superficial level. As I've said, what works for one, won't work for another—*ever*. Knowing how women work is going to give you the edge. However, trying to outguess her or play tricks on her or even using hypnosis will never work. Knowing why she does what she does is better than trying to outwit her. Don't ever try to one-up a woman. She will have your balls in no time flat. Remember she's got what you want and, therefore, the ball's in her court.

There are a few universal truths to what women really want from men. Most say that a nice smile, nice clothes and a clean body do the trick. Does he have to be handsome? No, not necessarily. But he does have to have a personality. There has to be *something* there for them to latch on to. If you give her a cardboard cutout of what you think she wants, she's going to see right through you. No amount of money or good clothing or pheromones are gonna save you. You were born with a distinct personality which you should never try to change. If you use it right, you can land the girl of your dreams. And by using it right, I mean, being man enough to *be* yourself. And if you give her yourself with those three elements I spoke of in the previous chapter, you are home-free.

WHAT WE LEARNED:
- Most myths about dating are bull.
- Stop thinking about myths and start concentrating on improving yourself.
- Most people who rely on myths are game players.

USE WHAT YOU'VE GOT

The best advice I, or anyone else for that matter, can give you is to use what you've got. Use what you've got and don't be afraid to do it. Maybe you're not the best looking guy but you have a big penis. That's always a crowd pleaser. Maybe you're cute but you have a crappy job. Maybe you get tongue-tied around women but you're working on a novel. Women eat that stuff right up. You're an artist? Hey, you've just written your own ticket. Maybe you're in some stupid garage band. Man, why are you reading this book? Women don't care if you're talented or not. As long as you're behind some instrument on some stage, you're sure to get laid sooner or later.

The point is to think of what you have. Right now. Stop and think. Okay. So you've got it. You can fix her computer if it tears up or you can change the oil in her car. Whatever it is, use it, work it to your advantage.

On the other hand, there is this thing called *Artificial Coolness* where some people act like they're a lot cooler than they are. Or maybe they pretend to have a lot of money or a cool job or whatever. Let me tell you one thing, chicks can and will see right through that. Never, ever pretend to be something you're not. No one likes a fake of any kind. Don't be a phony. It will come right back and bite you.

All you have to do is act like yourself. You have to accept yourself first before you can ask anyone else to accept you. So what if you're not where you wanted to be financially? So what if you haven't done the things you wanted to do? You will, in time. Just don't pretend to be something you're not.

Women are also interested in guys who do want to improve themselves and do more with their lives. The point is that you have to have something to offer a woman. You just have to do a little soul searching and find it. Everybody has something and if you can't find anything, you're not looking hard enough. If you have nothing to offer, then you're not going to get anything in return. What you give is what you get. Find out what you have and then get ready to offer it up.

You might even want to consider this. Lower your expectations. If the model doesn't want anything to do with you, why not go with the normal chick that hasn't been surgically enhanced? Sure, I know men want beautiful women with big boobs who can cook. And women want men who are rich, good looking and have a great sense of humor. No wonder we're all miserable. So why always go for the women you probably don't have a chance with? I'm not saying to date a woman with rotten teeth who is five hundred pounds overweight. I'm saying, don't overlook the good women out there who aren't built like a Barbie doll.

None of us are perfect, thank God. As with real beauty, real ugliness is rare. Today, it's all about the looks. But most of us look pretty good already. So do yourself a favor and stop comparing chicks with other chicks. Stop comparing them with models and Playmates and actresses. This is a very immature thing to do. You're not in junior high anymore. They are just like you: Ordinary people. And, for God's sake, if you have a ranking game with your buddies—the one where you rate chicks on a scale of one to ten—stop that. That is so crass and rude it's unbelievable. If a chick catches you doing it, you are toast. And you know what?

The only guys who do that are the ones who don't have a chance with any of the chicks they're ranking. It's nothing more than a way for them to put these girls down. Look at it like this: what would you think if a woman did this to you?

WHAT WE LEARNED:
- Use what you got.
- Never rate women on a scale of 1-10.

IT'S ALL ABOUT THE BENJAMINS

Have you ever heard that phrase—"Cheap with money, cheap with love"? It's true. In order to turn yourself into a dating machine, you are going to have to spend some bread. And when you get a girl, expect to spend even more. You don't have to be rich, but you need some cash so you don't come off looking like a cheapskate.

Keep in mind that most women do not want to be with a guy who won't spend a few bucks on her. If you can't afford a few dinners out and a bouquet of flowers from time to time...well, why bother?

So what if you don't have any cash right now? You've got a job, don't you? Right now start a "Dating Fund." Put a little money back every week for dating. Put it in a safe place and leave it alone. Once you're ready to go out there, you've got the cash you need and, believe me, you will need it. Women are expensive.

Now I know there are those of you who will read this and think all women are money-grubbing bitches and all they care about is how much money you've got. If so, you've got it all wrong. And, if this is the way you think, just know that you're not living in the real world. In the real world, this is how it really works. If you want to get a girlfriend, you need to know that you have to spend a little on her. I'm not saying to go in debt or anything, but if you can't spare a dinner out or a glass of wine or whatever, then maybe you're not ready to date. And that's okay. You don't have to. But if you know what you're up against, then you will be all the better.

You have to understand that women like to be treated like they are somebody special. Are you willing to treat her like that? So, even if she insists, do *not* let her pay for dinner. If you make her pay, this tells her that you're not really interested or you're just a dork who doesn't know any better. It makes her feel like crap and not at all special. Maybe this is a catch-22, but who said love was easy?

When a man doesn't want to pay for dinner, this tells a woman a lot of things. It tells her that if they got married, he would be the type of guy who asks why she needs so many shoes. And also, this sends a pretty clear signal that he can't afford to help her raise a family or even buy a house. Or that he'd be one of those fathers who makes his kids pick up cans off the side of the road.

Not a prospect many women want. She can afford her own dinner, you know?

This is not to say that you should go bankrupt in order to become a dating machine. In fact, if you do stuff that is out of your price range, your next date can't be at Burger King. Anything less than what you did on the first date will be a letdown.

So what can you do? Find stuff that's in your price range. Also, start your fund and keep a few dollars around in case you get lucky and get a date. Being prepared doesn't mean being cheap. However, if you can't afford a nice dinner, you are going to have to get creative and work a little harder. It'll be a pain in the butt, but worth it in the long run.

PLACES AND/OR THINGS YOU MIGHT DO ON THE CHEAP:

- You can cook for her at your place. Steaks don't cost that much.
- You can meet her in the park for a picnic. You can buy finger foods at the grocery store.
- You can see the matinee show at the movies or theatre.
- You can attend free outdoor concerts.
- You can window shop.
- You can write her poems about the lovely color of her hair.
- If you're a guitarist, you can play for her.
- You can go for long drives in your car.

If she likes you bunches, she isn't really going to care *where* you take her as long as you're a gentleman and pay for everything. But remember, if you're cheap, you're never going to get to see the inside of her bedroom. It's like this, dude: If you don't pay, she ain't gonna let you play. And I bet you're sick of playing with yourself.

WHAT WE LEARNED:
- It's never a good idea to be cheap.
- You don't have to be rich to date. Find inexpensive alternatives.

MIND YOUR MANNERS.

Your mother should have taught you better. Apparently, she didn't. That's why I'm here. Women like men with manners. Bad manners spell bad boyfriend. Simply put, when you look at her, you're looking at a good time in the sack. When she looks at you, she's usually looking for a potential boyfriend. And she doesn't want anything to do with you if you're bad boyfriend potential.

Bad boyfriend forgets to clean himself. He's weird and smelly and just plain bad news. You want to be good boyfriend. The upside? Good boyfriend always gets laid.

So what can you do? It's pretty easy to have good manners. Most of it is just common sense. Go ask Miss Manners if you have to. Watch some Martha Stewart or read a book on etiquette.

But there are a few little things that you should be aware of. And the most important thing you will read in this book or ever be told is: *Hold the door open for her.* And I repeat: *Hold the door open for her.*

I know when a guy doesn't do this, it spells loser to me. It's like he's getting ahead of himself and doesn't even know I'm there. I think, *How good is this guy going to be in bed if he isn't considerate enough to open the door for me?* So, if you do this, you are ahead of the game. Believe me, she will be impressed that you are that courteous.

HERE ARE A FEW OTHER THINGS YOU SHOULD KNOW:

- Again, open the door for her. Get a little ahead of her, open it and then let her enter first, following close behind, but not too close where you'll step on her heels.
- Open her car door *first.* Let her get inside, shut it and then go to your side. This spells gentleman and consideration. And that racks up major points with chicks.
- Never, ever, ever slam the door in her face. Even if you're mad at her.
- If you're going to a nice restaurant, pull the chair out for her and wait until she sits before you sit. How easy is that? Not that easy because I have witnessed many guys just plunking down before the chick even makes it to the table. Whenever I see this, I always think, *jerk.* So does she.
- Don't chew gum.
- Never burp. A girl I know told me, "I was out with this guy and out of nowhere, he burped. Not a little, oh-excuse-me kind of burp, but a loud raunchy burp. A stinky one! And the kicker is he didn't ask to be excused." Why would anyone do that? Beats me, but if you do it, plan on going home alone. Of course, once you start seeing someone on a regular basis, you might accidentally let out a burp or fart. Once you do, either apologize or laugh it off. We all burp and fart. Just not in the first, tentative stages.
- A word on cursing. I don't think you should jump right into it until you've felt her out a little. She could be one of those chicks who rarely curses and just doesn't see a need for "such" language. This doesn't mean she's necessarily a prude—it might be a good indicator, though—but it's a good idea to wait until she uses the first curse word. Regardless of how much she curses, don't overdo it and get crude. Remember, you're not around the boys. I know this is a double standard but she might sure her cursing as sassy and yours as threatening. She may have been brought up in a family where men don't curse around women.
- Don't throw a mad, hissy fit even if you stump your toe or catch your dick in your pants. (If you do, I do feel sorry for you.) Be a man about it and suffer in silence.

- If she does something to piss you off—chances are, at some point, she will—just grimace and let it go. You can call a buddy up later and vent. But, at first, do not throw a temper tantrum in front of her. It spells future wife beater.
- You're a bastard if... You get her drunk off her butt and take advantage of her. If you do this, you will rot in hell. That is so sleazy.
- Do not correct her spelling or pronunciation. *Don't correct her!* It's a one way ticket to hell. If she makes a jerk out of herself, let her. Or smile and think about how cute it is when she mispronounces something.
- Don't ever give her fashion tips. You are a dead man if you do. Remember, she's going to see you as a project regardless of whether you are or not. So nothing you say regarding fashion will have any validity. (Most women believe they're all fashion aficionados.)
- Don't ever ask if she's a real blonde, otherwise, you have zero chance of finding out for yourself, which, everyone knows, is much more fun.
- Don't ever ask about her shaving habits. (You know I'm not talking about her legs, don't you?)
- Don't ever disrespect her.
- Don't even think about ever hitting her. Otherwise, you might find yourself in jail. If she infuriates you this much, try some anger management courses and put a lid on it.
- Don't ever call or think she's a whore if you've just slept with her. If you think stuff like that, you've got issues and need to seek help ASAP.
- Don't ask, don't tell. Past sexual experiences should be kept in the past. More than likely she is probably more experienced than you want her to be. When it eventually comes up, just be happy that you're with a seasoned veteran. Virginity is highly overrated.
- Don't ever get her name wrong. Ask twice if you have to and memorize it, even ask her to spell it in case you're having trouble. If you pronounce it wrong, she will correct you. Take notes. (She is.)

These are just a few things you should know before you undertake dating. The more you know, the better off you'll be. In dating, it is *always* about the woman. Hard truth, but if you're too selfish and self-centered to learn this, you might always be alone. This is what all good daters know. Sure, you can have fun, too, but getting off on the wrong foot by forgetting something as small as opening the door for her spells disaster.

I know what you're thinking: *Why does stuff like this matter so much to chicks?* Who knows why? But it does. Always remember that it is you who is romancing her. It is you who is showing yourself to her to see if she likes. It is you who is on display. Play your cards right and you'll never get rid of her. And then you can be in charge a little.

Another important thing to do is to grow up. Immaturity won't cut it. Grow a pair for God's sake! Partying-and-having-a-good-time guy might go home with the bar slut, but he's not going to ever develop a real relationship.

WHAT WE LEARNED:
- Mind your manners. All women love men who have good manners.

TEETH

When was the last time you had your teeth cleaned, or for that matter, X-rayed? (Every six months is when you're *supposed* to do it.) If it's been a while, know that your choppers are one of the first things chicks will notice and that's because they know a man who takes good care of his teeth will also take good care of them.

I know some of you will read this and think, "This is just common sense." (What *is* it with the common sense thing?) However, let me just tell you that some men—perhaps not you, yourself—don't take care of their teeth. And teeth are something that can make or break a potential attraction. Say she looks over at you and sees something she likes. Say you come over to her and smile, showing not your pearly whites but some hillbilly-looking teeth. Do you get my drift? If you don't take care of your teeth that tells her you probably don't take care of a lot of other things. So, don't be flippant about this subject. It is very important.

Keep in mind that if you take care of these little things, she's going to have no reason to turn you down. More importantly, she's going to have no reason to try and change you. (Yeah, right. She will always try to change you because that's what women do.) But the point is, don't give her anything to start with. Make her work to change you. Improve on yourself first before she even gets in the picture and she'll wonder how she got so lucky. She'll tell her girlfriends, "I don't know why, but there's nothing wrong with this guy! I mean, can there be *nothing* wrong with him? His teeth are good, he has great manners and he always holds the door open for me. Am I just being paranoid?"

Now, take a good look at your teeth in the mirror. Are they stained? Are some missing? If so, get an appointment with a dentist and get all that nasty work done. You want to keep your teeth in tip-top shape; otherwise, you'll have to get dentures on down the road.

It's also a good idea to whiten your teeth. You can start by using whitening toothpaste. If you've got the cash, have the dentist do it. If you can afford it, get your choppers fixed if you've got a few snaggles here and there. Some women don't mind teeth that are slightly crooked, but if they're so bad you look like an extra in an hillbilly movie, please do yourself a favor and get this done.

You may be saying, *Is there anything women don't notice?* And the answer is, no. there's not. Good luck to you, though.

WHAT WE LEARNED:
- Everything is important to women and that includes your teeth. Be sure to get your pearly whites in tip-top shape.

BE PREPARED

There are a few universal truths to what all women want. Ready for them?

WHAT SHE WANTS:
- For you to be perfect.
- To change you. (She will try.)
- Marriage. I don't care what she says, she usually wants marriage. All women do. The only exception to this is if she's

been married before or burned by man. Or if she's a lesbian and we all know lesbians only want to marry one another.

- Babies. This is one of her major life goals. (An exception: She already has babies and doesn't want any more.)

You have been warned. Do not proceed if any of this makes you break into hives.

BAD REPUTATION

You might not give a damn about your bad rep—in fact, you're probably proud of it—but she sure as hell cares about hers. She doesn't want anything to mess with her chances of getting a good guy and, eventually, a good husband. She also doesn't want you to think she's some kind of slut. Even if she is easy, she doesn't want anyone *else* to think it.

I once knew a guy who had a really good first date with a chick and then he jumped the gun and asked her, "So can I stay over at your place tonight?" And he wondered why she turned cold after that. I told him, "It's really simple, stupid. One of the biggest dating rules is that you never ask a chick if you can stay at her place. Whatever chance you had just went down the tubes. Why? Because, after you say something like that, she thinks you think she's a cheap ho and that makes her feel bad about herself."

Don't ever invite yourself to her place. Ever, even if you're getting "vibes" that she wants you to stay over. If she wants this, she will let your know. There will be *no* shadow of doubt. She doesn't want you to think that she's "easy" and if you ask this dumb question, that's precisely what you're telling her you think of her. You're telling her that all you're interested in is sex.

Believe me, once you let a woman know this, she will turn ice cold. It's true. Yes, it *is*. It might not make sense, but I know women think in these terms. Even if she's forty years old, she's still concerned with getting a bad reputation. Always wait for an invite! *Always!* Never, ever invite yourself up to some chick's pad! It will get you a one-way ticket to nowhere.

Now you can invite her to *your* pad, but do it nicely, "I have some really good gin at my place. Want to come up for a drink? You know, just a drink. I would love to keep talking to you."

I know that your mind is going to be on sex the entire evening, but never let *her* know it is. And when you invite her, don't think you're going to get lucky.

On the other hand, if she thinks you're not that interested in sex, she's going to want to know why. *Why doesn't he desire me? I've got to figure this guy out.* Coming on too strong with a lady is going to get you a ticket home—alone. Holding back and letting her come to you might just be your ticket to a night of wild monkey sex.

Let me reiterate. The more you act like you're not interested in sex, the stronger she will come on to you. Don't ever show that's all you're interested in—we all know it is—until she comes to you. Don't ever assume that she wants it. She might, but if you tell her you know what she's thinking, she's going to turn cold.

What if you do screw up and do something like the idiot I mentioned above? Claim stupidity. Tell her that you're drunk. That you didn't mean it. Tell her you were only joking. Laugh it off. Say you're sorry and if you still have a chance, she'll let you know. And move on to another subject quickly. Women do have long memories but if you brush it off, she may brush it off as well because she'll be embarrassed. And the reason she'll be embarrassed is because she'll think *she's* the one jumping the gun.

One of the most important things you can do is to *think before you speak.* She's keeping score, believe me.

WHAT WE LEARNED:
- Women do care about their reputations.
- Women don't want you or anyone else to think they're a cheap ho.
- Never invite yourself to her place.
- Invite her to your place only if you get the vibe she's digging you.

YOUR MUSIC

If you have the opportunity to bring a good looking girl home, you need some good tunes to help woo her. Take a good, hard look at your CD collection. Teenybopper music? *Kenny G?!* Oh, good

Lord! Hide those CDs or throw them away, which is even better. Get some rock-n-roll—Stones or Led Zeppelin or something with a little soul. Women usually love oldies and Otis Redding is always, always good. Women swoon when they hear him. (I know I do.) You might also want to get some Patsy Cline. I know it's country, but Patsy is just so good. You should already have some Dean Martin and Frank Sinatra in your collection. You do, right?

Remember, good music is the best music to set the stage. Get some music that shows you're a suave, sophisticated guy, not some redneck or dork. If you don't know where to start, that geek in the record store will.

WHAT WE LEARNED:
- Keep some good music around that will set the stage and let her know how cool you are.
- If you don't have any good music, get some.
- If you don't know where to start, start with the classics: Dean, Frank, Elvis, Beatles, etc.
- If you still don't know where to start, ask the geek at the record store. (Make sure he's not wearing a Metallica t-shirt, though.)

ME TARZAN—YOU JANE

No. No. No.

This may work in the movies but in real life, women rarely respond to a cave man/Tarzan mentality. If you try to woo her by beating your fists on your chest, expect her to call the cops. I know I would. *This guy is crazy!* You may be bigger, stronger and faster than she is, but she doesn't give a flying fig. (Neither does anyone else.)

You're not a male chauvinist pig, are you? If so, you are going to have a hard time hooking up. If you think that a woman's place is in the kitchen, why are you even bothering? Women expect and demand respect. If you aren't willing to give it to her, go buy a blow-up doll to be your girlfriend. She won't contradict you. And she's always available.

Another thing: Never alpha male a woman! By this I mean, don't push her around and don't try to "control" her in any way. I have seen this happen and it just makes me cringe. Never try to get the upper hand. I would hope that you would want to be on equal-footing with a chick and she you. But if you try to show your manliness by pushing her around, you just blew your chances.

Keep in mind that trust is the key. You have to let her know that if you two get behind closed doors you're not going to do anything bad. You are a lot bigger than her and she *has* to feel safe with you. You have to be trustworthy and the thing is, you either are or you aren't. Most people can pick up on this trait pretty quickly. If she gets bad vibes of any kind, she's gone. It's a protective measure. Do what you have to do to let her know she can trust you. Building trust takes time but know that it is a very necessary step if you want to succeed with women.

WHAT WE LEARNED:
- Me Tarzan, you Jane never works.
- Never alpha male a female, i.e., never push her around.
- If you're a male chauvinist pig, you need to change your attitude.

NEVER LET HER SEE YOU CRY LIKE A BABY

If you ask me, there is way too much male crying going on these days. You can't turn on the TV without seeing it. It's all over the movies. I mean, if something tragic has happened, by all means, cry your little heart out. But if you just found out your favorite TV show is going off the air, don't do it in front of her.

This is one of the myths that I think started in the seventies—the "All women like men who aren't afraid to cry" myth. Now every man out there is crying. You can't turn the TV on without seeing one blubbering away. And usually they're crying for stupid reasons, because they haven't been sensitive *enough* or something just as mundane. Truthfully, this makes us look like a nation of crybabies.

While it may be true that women like men to be a bit sensitive, they do not like crybabies. Remember, just like you have opinions on how women should act, they too have opinions on how men should act.

Life's a bitch.

On the other hand, expect *her* to cry. Be the shoulder she cries on. Women love to cry, it makes them feel good, it's cathartic. Just keep in mind that she's allowed to cry because she's a girl.

Also, God forbid if you should start talking about your feelings on the first few dates. Keep in mind that, at first, she won't care about your feelings. Feelings about the world and the beautiful sun and all that should be kept in check at first. Remember, she's looking for a man, but not a pansy. She doesn't want you to be soft. Therefore, until you've dated for a while, refrain from talking about your feelings. It's tacky and just a little bit creepy.

On the other hand, if she asks you to open up, open up—a little. Give her a story from your childhood that you remember fondly. *Don't* tell her about the time you were beaten up on the school bus.

One last thing—if you want to share your poetry, please don't. You should know why.

WHAT WE LEARNED:
- Cry only if something tragic happens, not at the beautiful sunset.
- Share your "feelings" only after you've been seeing someone for a while.
- If you do open up, give only a little—preferably funny—story. Don't bore her with tiny details.
- If she cries, be her shoulder.
- Poetry is a big no-no.

THE PRICE OF BEAUTY

Women spend so much time keeping themselves in shape its unreal. We spend hours jogging and lifting weights and thinking about that damned piece of chocolate cake we passed up at lunch. Why do we do it? Because we want to look good for the opposite sex. We know the better we look physically, the more potential mates we can attract. How many potential mates do you want to attract? If you want to attract a lot, maybe it's time to get in shape.

I won't go into detail about how you can get in shape, as there are many magazines, TV shows and sites on the internet devoted to this. The best advice I can offer you is to look in the mirror, assess your physical situation and then do something about it. If you have a few pounds to lose, lose them. If you need to work on your abs, work on your abs. Getting into shape isn't rocket science, believe me, but staying out of shape might keep you on the bench and never getting the chance to bat.

I know it's hard to get in shape, but such is the price of beauty. However, if you want to land hot chicks, it's a good idea to look hot yourself. And the easiest way to do that is to get in shape. (It's a good idea to see your doctor and get his okay first.) And everyone can do this.

If you need to lose some weight, simply cut back on your calorie intake. That's all it takes—watching what you eat.

WHAT WE LEARNED:
- If you're overweight, lose it.
- Women love hard bodies. Turn yourself into a hard body—but not a bodybuilder—and you shouldn't have any trouble hooking up.

SHARP DRESSED MAN

Women spend a huge amount of money on new clothing. If you knew how much, you would appreciate them all the more. And you would wonder how they can afford it. Two words: Credit cards. It's true. Women are going in debt to look nice for you. That's how important it is to them. They put *a lot* of time into the way they look.

If you want to stand out in the crowd and attract lots of potential mates, one quick and easy way to do it is to dress nice. You don't want to jeopardize your chances of getting lucky because you were dressed sloppy. Sometimes, all chicks will give you is *one glance.* That first impression is very crucial. If they don't like what they see, they are not going to give you the time of day.

Here is a list of what to wear. You don't have to spend a weeks' pay, either. Just add a few items weekly until you have a nice, new wardrobe. If you are uncertain about what items to purchase, the help of a sales associate can do wonders. But keep this list in mind.

FASHION DOS AND DON'TS:

- *Pants:* Flat-fronted slacks are the best. They are also the most stylish. I don't have to tell you these pants need to be in a solid color, do I? Okay, buy pants in a solid color. No stripes or plaids allowed. Black, gray, and khaki are the best colors.

- *Shirts.* Solid color button-down shirts in a good cotton material. You can also find some that are cotton/poly blended that look great. No crazy stripes or patterns. Just plain shirts that will go well with your pants. Also, Hawaiian shirts should be reserved for special occasions. Like going to Hawaii.

- *Sweaters.* Lightweight material in solid colors. A crew-neck or v-neck is good and should always be worn with a white t-shirt underneath. (Think Gap or Banana Republic.)

- *Belts.* Belt color must match shoe color. Hopefully, neither will be in white.

- *Undershirts.* White, all cotton t-shirts that should be unstained. Wear them under all shirts. You can also wear those wife-beater shirts under your shirts. As long as you're not a wife-beater, that is. (Wash them separately and use a little bleach which will keep them looking whiter for longer.)

- *Underwear.* Boxers or boxer-briefs are the best. (Going commando isn't recommended.)

- *Socks.* No white socks unless you are wearing jeans or khakis. Colored—black, brown, tan—socks for all other pants. And no argyles. Any socks with pills on them or holes should be thrown out.

- *Holes.* In fact, anything that has holes the manufacturer didn't put in should be thrown out, as well as anything that is stained or ragged. If you have any doubt about something, throw it out.

- *Coats.* A good leather coat—in black or dark brown but preferably in black—is a good investment and can be worn with anything. Make sure it is in a classic style and if you buy a motorcycle jacket, be sure to have a motorcycle. (Note that these jackets are not recommended.) You might also want to get a wool or wool-blended jacket that zips or buttons down. These are good in black and should hit around the hip area or a little below. Please do not ever wear a duster coat of any kind unless you are mounting a horse.

- *Hats.* No. Just forget about hats. Unless you are a biker, rapper or tattoo artist, don't wear a skull hat. In fact, the only time you should wear a hat is if you're going: Hunting, hiking, beaching.

- *Wallets.* You need a nice, leather one that doesn't close with Velcro. It should also be free of thousands of little useless papers and your CPR card that ran out two years ago.

- *Man bags.* No man bags or messenger bags unless you are traveling or going to school, on vacation, or, obviously, going to work.

- *Eyeglasses.* No aviator-style glasses. If you can swing it, get some contacts. If you have to wear glasses, or prefer to, go shopping and see what's in style and buy a new, stylish pair. Nothing says smart man quite like a smart pair of glasses. (Yes, just like men love women with glasses, women love men with glasses. Correction: Men with stylish glasses.)

- *Watches.* A watch is for telling time. Any other device on a watch besides telling time makes one look like a dork. Any nice watch with a leather band will do—a tank watch is always good. Also, a watch in stainless steel always looks classic.

- *Shoes.* Let's stop for a minute and talk about shoes. I don't think you can begin to understand how important shoes are to women. Again, women are in debt because of shoes. Do you know that many women have been known to pay as much as five-hundred—and up!—bucks for a single pair of shoes? Yeah, it's true. One of the first things the ladies will look at is your shoes. I don't know why this is, but you can tell so much about a person by just looking at their shoes. You need good shoes. Bypass Foot Locker and go to a men's shoe store. Look over what they have. If any of these shoes have a tassel, bypass them as well. Still not sure which ones to get? A good indicator is if you think a TV preacher—or a salesman—might wear them. If so, bye-bye. Good shoes have a slightly thicker sole and they are also made of leather—*real* leather. They can be in brown or black. (Unless you're a pimp, never buy a pair of shoes in any other color.) You don't have to buy five or six pairs, just one good pair to keep for your dates. Always clean the dust and grime off your shoes and sometimes shine them. Buy a shoe-shining kit if you have to.

If you still need help, look around at a few men who have some style and check out their shoes. If you're still in doubt, like I said, ask a sales associate to help you. Buying a nice pair of leather shoes in a classic style is the best way to go. (These kinds of shoes usually do not have hiking boot bottoms, nor are they hiking boots. Sorry.) You can wear these shoes with jeans or khakis or dress slacks.

The point of all this is that you want to make a good first impression. Chicks will judge you on your appearance. It may not be right and it may not be fair, but that's life. You want them to notice *you,* not your clothes.

You want to look hip and stylish but never—never!—sleazy. No gold chains or pinky rings—unless you are wearing a suit and your boss has just called you to unload some stuff off the back of a truck. And, if you're not in a rock band, no earrings. Yup, you heard me right. Get rid of it now. (If you have a nose ring or any other kind of ring somewhere on your body, I am assuming you work in a tattoo parlor. If so, keep up the good work.)

You say, *All this sounds good but I have no idea where to start.* If so, study the good men's magazines (not *Juggs*) and see what's in style. Tear a few of those pics out and take them with you when you go to shop. Also, try everything on. Bend down and over and hug yourself to make sure the seams don't creak. Check out the sleeves. They should cover your wrists when you hold your arm out straight—think about reaching for the biscuits. If you reach and your sleeve comes up over your wrist a little too far, it's too small.

Check out the hemline on your pants as well. It should drape around the top of your shoes but never above your ankle. You want clothing to fit but never skin tight. A little looser is better than a little tighter, unless, of course, you're a stripper and if you are, I shouldn't have to tell you anything about picking up chicks.

Buy the stuff *as you can afford it.* If you're strapped for cash, set a few bucks back every week until you have enough for one good outfit, from head to toe. Then, save some more and buy another and another. Soon, your closet will have admiring glances from all the ladies who are about to enter your life. Just don't be afraid to change your wardrobe. Be a sharp dressed man. Looking good and having good clothing is so going to boost your confidence level. And that's what we're after here. Once you have confidence, you can conquer the world.

WHAT WE LEARNED:
- The way a man dresses is very important to a woman. She will pick out a sharp dressed man in any crowd.
- Buy new, stylish clothes that make you look great. See list.
- If you can't afford new clothes, start a clothing fund today.

GROOMING

How you groom yourself leads one to believe that you care about the way you look. In turn, this makes others care about getting to know you better.

How's your hair doing? Is it funny looking? Weird? Chopped up? Is some of it missing? If you don't have a good haircut, it's time, my friend, to get that head of yours in as good as shape as your body and wardrobe.

Stop going to the barbershop. Old men don't care how you look, they're just thinking about how they're gonna spend that seven bucks you're gonna give them for making a mess of your hair. It's recommended that you get yourself an appointment with a stylist that can do something with your hair. They can give your various options about different men's styles.

If you're losing your hair, you might want to consider shaving it all off and going bald. Nothing raises eyebrows quite like a comb-over. Forget hair pieces, too, because anyone with a brain can detect one. Bald heads these days seem to be chick magnets. (Girls *love* to rub bald heads for some reason.) Remember, it's not the hair that attracts women, it's the confidence.

Now take a look at your face. First off, the unibrow. Unless you belong to a British band popular in the nineties, it ain't gonna work for you. (Maybe not even then.) Anyway, while you're getting your hair cut, ask the stylist to wax—not shave!—your unibrow. It's *not* an unmanly thing to do.

Very important note: If your stylish wants to "shape" your eyebrows, tell them no. Men that shape their eyebrows look odd, so don't do it. Pluck a few strays here and there, but that's all. Besides the unibrow, of course. You can get rid of all of it.

Now let's move on to shaving. You guys should *always* shave your faces if you plan on doing any kissing. Women do not like to be rubbed raw by a five o'clock shadow. Let me tell you how it feels. Go grab a piece of sandpaper. Rub it as hard as you can across your forehead. Ouch!

Do you have a beard? *Why do you have a beard?* Are you a lumberjack? If not, consider shaving it off. Women like to *see* men's faces. Beards *hide* men's faces. Get my drift?

If you have a moustache, you need to realize that they are out of fashion and every woman in the world is praying they never come back. That's not to say they won't be back in a few millennia's, but hey, if you're willing to wait it out, that's your business.

I'm not even going to say a word about soul patches and Elvis-sized sideburns. And that's because I shouldn't have to.

Let's turn our focus to cologne. All you need is a touch of this stuff. If you wear too much, she'll *really* get a headache. So, put a little dab on your hands, rub your hands together, and lightly slap it on. Never overpower anyone with your cologne. You want her to remember you, not your scent.

Keep in mind that the more attention you pay to yourself, the more confident you will be. And, as I have been saying, confidence is what we're after here, in case you haven't been paying attention. And, no, I'm not trying to turn you into a metrosexual.

WHAT WE LEARNED:
- Keep yourself properly groomed.
- Get a good haircut.
- Just a touch of cologne is all you need.

YOUR PAD

Now let's take a look at your pad. Oh, boy, this is going to be hard. For some reason—and I think it's because mom always picked up after her boy—men don't get cleaning. Not only that, they don't understand why women don't like dirty apartments. "It's not *that* bad," you say.

Look around your pad. If it's, to put it nicely, filthy, then you might want to consider doing something about it. One of the worst things you can do is ask a chick over and allow her to see your dirty house. Why? Because she's probably going to run if you do.

If you can't torch the place and start over, you are going to have to clean like crazy and do a little shopping. If you can afford it, hire a maid to swing by once a week. If not, start with the small things. The dirty dishes, for instance. Make it a habit to always clean up after yourself. Everything should be sparkling clean and all that clutter sitting around should be disposed of.

Think clean, uncluttered and nice. If you can afford a new couch, buy one with some style and get rid of that ugly one your granny gave you to get it out of her house. And don't forget to dust your big screen TV.

A LIST OF VERY IMPORTANT THINGS:
- Clean bed sheets. If you can afford it, the higher the thread-count the better. 300-plus is always good but if you go higher, she will never want to get out of bed. (A note on silk or satin sheets—don't. You will slide right off them. Cotton is always best.)
- Toilet paper in the bathroom. Also, a good, clean toilet. Clean, clean, clean! A good, clean bathtub in case you get into the shower together. Also, clean towels so you can dry her off afterwards. It wouldn't hurt to replace that bathmat, either. You do have a bathmat, don't you?
- Everything in the kitchen should be clean and rodent/pest free. If you have cockroaches, get the problem taken care of.
- A nice bottle of champagne in the fridge. Don't open it unless she comes over. Maybe have a few nice snacks on hand, too. (And I don't mean Cheese Whiz.)
- How about buying some special blend coffee? I think you should.
- A nice set of silverware. (No plastic spoons!)
- A nice set of dishes and good, thick glasses that are not plastic.

Get it done and get on with your life. You don't want to spend too much time on this. Take one day a week to do all the necessary cleaning and the rest of the week, practice your new dating skills.

WHAT WE LEARNED:
- No woman wants to visit a man who lives in a pigsty.
- Clean your pad.
- Always have toilet paper on hand.

BEFORE YOU VENTURE OUT…

Okay, so you're ready now, aren't you? But, before you step out that door and venture into the big, scary world of trying to find yourself a nice girl to spend some time with, it's a good idea check yourself. This is to ensure that your appearance is as good as it can be. You don't want to make a bad first impression because you didn't take time to brush your teeth.

BEFORE YOU GO OUT, BE SURE TO:
- Shower.
- Shave or trim facial hair.
- Floss and brush your teeth and use mouthwash. Don't forget to gargle.
- Check for any stray hairs in nose or ears.
- Iron clothes.
- Shine shoes.
- Trim and file nails, fingers *and* toes. (You never know, you might get lucky and you don't want to gouge her with your sharp toenails, do you?)

If you look your best, chicks will see you at your best. They will see *you* and chances are they will like what they see. And that's the impression you want. Don't sabotage yourself before you even get to the date by not taking time to look your best. *Take time to do this.* It shows the ladies that you care about yourself and that will make them want to care about getting to know you better. This stuff will become a habit and soon, you won't want to leave your place without looking your best.

WHAT WE LEARNED:
- Always groom yourself properly before you hit the door.
- Look in the mirror and make sure everything looks okay.

GOOD TASTE

It's good to know that women like men with good taste, whether it's in cars, wine or clothing. Again, it's the James Bond thing. He has it going on. He knows how to work chicks like nobody's business. Of course, he's a fictitious character but you can still learn a thing or two from him.

Shocking to know, but it is possible to be interested in more than the sports page or the big game. You can cultivate good taste by reading, watching other people, traveling, surfing the internet, watching good documentaries, and studying different cultures. (If you watch documentaries, you'll always have something to talk about on dates.) Take a stroll in a museum every once in a while. Open a book and the world opens up to you. Don't just read comic books, read Bukowski, Fitzgerald, Keroauc and, of course, the other basic classics. You'll be surprised how good they are. Watch classic movies like *Alfie* and *La Dolce Vita*. Cultivate a thirst for knowledge on all subjects. Don't just see the world around you; see the world outside of the one you live. Another way to put this: Think outside the box.

Another thing to notice about Mr. Bond is this: He loves women. You have to love women in order to be good with them. Think about the old masters: Dean Martin, Sinatra, Elvis. They all have something in common and it's simple. They loved women, each and every one of them. They didn't discriminate. They loved all women of all shapes and sizes. If you love women, half the work is already done. And by love I mean, you are fascinated by women. They make you smile. If you're misogynous—which means you hate women—no amount of work is going to help you. And if you are misogynous, you need some help.

WHAT WE LEARNED:
- Women love men with good taste. Cultivate it.
- Think outside the box.
- Don't be misogynous.

BE A MAN

Just a quick note on this. If any sort of confrontation happens where the woman you're with is in some sort of trouble, be a man and defend her honor. Stick up for her even if it's just telling some jerk to step back. You will find that the more beautiful your honey is, the more likely she is gonna get hit on. You don't want some jerk taking your place before you even get started.

One thing to remember, though, is that if the guy is bigger than you, just try to solve the problem by having a little talk. If you do get into a fight and he beats the crap out of you, don't say I didn't warn you. And don't ever pick fights to show her how strong you are. Just show her when and if the time comes.

Added bonus: It is a huge aphrodisiac for women to see their man stick up for them. She will be all over you once it's over. *He can protect me! He stood up for me! I love him soooo much! He is so getting laid tonight!*

WHAT WE LEARNED:
- Be the man and you might just get yourself a sex kitten.
- Try to work out any problems with talk first.

BITCHY-BEAUTIFUL GIRLS

Don't you just love 'em? They got it goin' on! They are the best. They know how to dress that tight little body of theirs to make your jaw drop. They also know how to crush you like a bug. So, this begs the question: Are all beautiful women bitches? As always, it depends on the girl. And it depends on her circumstances.

A girl can be bitchy-beautiful because some jerk hurt her once. A girl can be bitchy-beautiful because her daddy gave her everything and told her she was a princess. Regardless, now the rest of the world has to suffer.

Having said that, let me say this: Never, *ever* let a woman demean you. I don't care how pretty she is, she's not worth it. Once you do, she's got your balls and you really need them for yourself. Stand up to chicks like this. Remember that no chick wants a wimp and if she's testing you and you fail, she will consider you a wimp. Who wants to be a wimp?

How will you know if she's testing you? She may do odd things like ask you to dance with a gay guy or give her a lap dance or ask you to take your shirt off at a club. Anything that is a little weird or unmanly, don't do. Remember, she's just testing you to see if she can push you around. Don't let her.

Another word on beautiful but not necessarily bitchy girls: Just because she looks like she is out of your league doesn't necessarily mean she is. She could have been raised in a trailer and have no self confidence. She could be waiting on someone to talk to *her.* If you like her, why not give it a try? All she can do is say no and you won't have to spend the rest of your life asking yourself, "Why didn't I ask her out?" She might say yes. But then again, she might say no. However, with all the confidence you've acquired thus far, your fear of getting turned down should start diminishing.

WHAT WE LEARNED:
- Bitchy, beautiful girls can be a pain in the butt. Make sure she's worth it.
- Just because she's beautiful doesn't mean she gets asked out all the time. Why not try? All she can do is say no. If she does, move on and don't let it bother you at all.

A WORD ON AGGRESSIVE GIRLS

Yes, they are out there. They do exist. There are girls who come on strong, hit hard and then hit the door. We will kindly refer to them as the *aggressive girls.*

Some men can handle the aggressive girl and some can't. If you decide you'd like to get to know her better, hang on. It's going to be a bumpy ride.

If you're lucky enough to hook up with an aggressive girl, all you need to know is that she will make the first move and she will be in totally in control. All you have to do is wait. Hopefully, you won't get hurt. Just watch yourself, though. Aggressive girls tend to drink a lot. And, yeah, they can drink you under the table. Keep an eye on how much *you're* drinking so you don't miss out on your opportunity to have a wild, crazy night. But don't expect to see her in the morning.

Should you hook up with one of them, pat yourself on the back. She will more than likely take care of everything and if she doesn't like you, she'll let you know and not waste your time. But don't think that because she's coming on strong that she's a ho-bag. This means, if she's coming on strong, she might just be playing you. Which means, you might get lucky and you might not. It all depends on her mood at the time. That's just her personality shining through. Not all people are meek and mild, thank God.

How to spot an aggressive girl? Look for her to be dancing on the tables. She'll be the loud one having the most fun at any party. Amble on up to her and let the rest take care if itself. (Also note that if she's aggressive in the club or bar, she'll be aggressive in the sack. If this intimidates you in the least, keep your distance. She won't let you say no.)

WHAT WE LEARNED:
- Aggressive girls can be fun.
- Maybe you'll get lucky enough and come across one.

BASIC RULES OF ATTRACTING WOMEN

Someone once told me they ask every girl out they see. Why? I don't know, but I guess the dude thought the law of averages was on his side. The more he asked out, the more likely he was going to hook up. The only problem was that he looked a little *too* desperate. Never show desperation. Don't be stupid. Don't act stupid. If she doesn't want you, let it go and be gracious. This is a basic rule of attracting women. Let's go over a few more.

THE BASIC RULES OF ATTRACTING WOMEN:
- *Let her come to you.* That's right, let her come to you. You can give her the "eye" or maybe a smile or even send her a drink. But if she doesn't give you the signal to approach, leave her alone. If she does give you the signal, then it's all up to you. So, you have to wait for the signal to approach.
- Women are in control. You are not and you never will be. You can whine, "But I saw this guy in a bar approaching

women and getting hit on left and right." Some men just know how to play it better. If you watched closely, he lets the women do all the touchy-feely at first. Later on, he can get touchy-feely when she invites him back to her crib. Never do the touchy-feely with a woman you've just met. Let *her* do it.

- Women like men who are comfortable with themselves.
- Women want men who are both physically and emotionally strong. The stronger you are, the stronger her babies will be. That's the reason. It's true. It's all about Natural Selection. She probably doesn't even realize this, but it's a basic biological fact.
- Be the guy who is willing to rise to the challenge to be a better mate, a better partner.
- Women like men who are good listeners and who ask questions about them.

Now that we've got that out of the way, let's move on to another subject. And this subject is about assumptions. Whenever you are dealing with women, it's good to not make any assumptions about them. If they turn you down, take it like a man and move on. But, most importantly, don't make any assumptions about her.

DON'T MAKE ASSUMPTIONS ABOUT HER BEING:
- A slut.
- A whore.
- Any other bad word you can think of to make yourself feel better about being turned down.
- A homemaker.
- A home wrecker.
- A bitch.

THE PICK-UP ARTIST

I shouldn't have to say this, but I am going to. If you think you have a great pick-up line, keep it to yourself. Pick-up lines never, ever work on chicks. You will get a "Loser!" or an eye roll whenever you attempt one.

But how *do* you approach her? How do you know *when* to approach her? Watch for the signals.

SIGNALS:
- A smile thrown in your direction.
- A coy look.
- She runs her hands through her hair.
- She's staring at you and when you look at her, she looks away almost in embarrassment, like you caught her staring. (Which, of course, you *did*.)
- She sends you a drink.
- She bites her lips or licks her lips.
- She jerks her head for you to come over.

Now that you have the signal, it's time to move in. As you approach her, remember, she's just as nervous as you are, if not more so. Put her at ease by being a gentleman and by giving her a nice smile.

WHAT WOMEN THINK WHEN THEY FIRST ZONE IN ON A GUY:
- "He better do something to impress me."
- "He looks good."
- "I want to turn him down, but maybe I should give him a chance."
- "I wish he'd do something to let me know he likes me."
- "God, I hope I don't make a fool of myself."
- "I feel very shy and nervous all of a sudden."
- "Oh, no, here he comes. What can I do? Act like I don't care. Yeah, that's good."
- "Oh, damn it, I just giggled."
- "If he comes on too strong, I am going to get pissed off."
- "Why does he keep looking over here and not doing anything?"
- "Well, if he's coming over, I wish he'd hurry. I don't have all night!"

- "I hope he's nice and doesn't use any pick-up lines."
- "Oh, God! Here he comes! Be calm, be calm!"
- "Yeah, he looks nice. Good shoes! If he asks for my number, I will probably give it to him."

She wants you to impress her, but she doesn't want you to know you've impressed her. Keep in mind that you're starting off as friends. Oh, no, the dreaded friend zone! *Yes.* If you think like this and get your dirty little mind off sex, then your chances of scoring are increased. Why? She automatically thinks that you want to have sex and she's not easy. If you put *her* in the friend zone first, she'll be dying to get out of it. So, therefore, put her in the friend zone and more than likely, you will find yourself out of it.

So, once you get the signal, walk over and say, "Hi, how's it going?" She will smile or nod or say something. Then say, "Hey, I'm _____. And you are?"

Asking her name is important because it forces her to tell you who she is and opens the conversation. Sure, you will be nervous and maybe stumble over your words, but the point is to try and get to know her. Once you go up to her and introduce yourself, let *her* talk to *you*. The rest, if you act cool, is going to take care of itself.

The point is to improvise in conversation. Just let whatever happens happen. Don't put too much time or thought into what you're going to say as it will come off as staged. Keep in mind that she's a normal person and talking to her shouldn't be any different than talking to any other person you don't already know.

If it's awkward when you do approach her—or, perhaps you've misread the signal—just say, "Well, nice talking to you," and walk away. Always be a gentleman. More than likely, this will make her feel bad for being a bitch.

REMEMBER IF SHE REJECTS YOU, SHE MIGHT JUST BE:
- Involved in a relationship already.
- Married with kids.
- A lesbian.
- Heartbroken over some other guy.
- Just plain mean and miserable.

Rejection doesn't always have to do with you, you know? There are extenuating circumstances. She might like you but because she's got some baggage, she can't go out with you.

It's also good to keep in mind that this woman isn't necessarily going to change your world. She might be shallow. She might steal your stereo. She might not be worth it once you've gotten to know her. But you need to try. Expend some effort and you should get something in return. Expend nothing and get nothing.

One more note. Before you approach her—or any other woman for that matter—make sure she isn't already taken. If you have no way of finding out, look for a ring of some sort. A big diamond is a good indicator some other guy already has his hooks in her. Also, a wedding ring should speak volumes. If you have no way of telling, go ahead and talk to her, then slip it in, easy-like, "You don't have a boyfriend, do you?"

There you go. You will find out and you can move on with your life. And if she does have a boyfriend and is thinking about dumping him, you can move in and snatch her right up. Warning: *Said boyfriend might be a jealous freak who might come after you. Make sure she's worth it!*

WHAT WE LEARNED:
- Before you approach any woman, make sure she's available.
- Women are just as nervous as you are when they meet someone new.
- Never use lame pick-up lines.
- Rejection isn't always about you.

I'VE GOT A CRUSH ON YOU

Maybe you don't want a stable of beautiful women. Maybe you have your eye on someone in particular. She works where you do or she's the clerk at the video store or she's a stripper at your local club. Wherever she is, you want her and you want her bad. She's gorgeous. She has the perfect body and…

Anyway. Take a good look at the woman of your dreams. You're thinking that you don't have a chance with her and that you might as well throw in the towel and give this one up. She might not be interested in a guy like you. She *might* be out of your league.

You know what? She might not be.

If you've been reading this book so far and have followed my advice, it shouldn't shock you to know you've got a good chance with this chick. And why shouldn't you? You're in good shape, you dress well, you have good manners and you are prepared to kick some guy's butt if he messes with her.

Before you ask her out, why not start a dialogue with her? Whenever you see her, smile and say hello. Doing this a few times allows you to develop rapport. As long as you approach her with a smile, she should smile in return. She's going to know what's up, believe me.

If she returns your smile and engages in your conversations, something about you impresses her. And how will you know?

LOOK FOR SIGNS:
- Have you caught her staring at you, then looking away quickly?
- Has she given you a shy, small smile?
- Has she ever tapped you on the shoulder or touched your arm?
- Has she ever told you a joke?
- Has she done anything to indicate there's an interest?

If you're getting these signs, go ahead and ask her out.

HERE'S A FEW EXAMPLES OF WHAT TO SAY:
- "Hey, do you want to get a bite to eat after work?"
- "I was thinking that we could go out sometime, if you like."
- "Have you heard about the concert series in the park? Would you like to go with me?"
- "How about a cup of coffee?"

Ask her, set the date—like, "How about next week, on Wednesday around seven?"—and be on your way. Also, you want her to know you're interested, but at the same time, don't come on too strong. Wait and listen to what she's saying.

It is important to note that you should apply these same rules to any situation. It's always "Proceed with caution" with any woman because you never know how they'll react. Look for signs. If she's smiling and being friendly that's always a good indicator she likes you. If, however, she runs away and avoids you, it's not.

Another word on women you work with. This is definitely "proceed with caution" because of all that sexual harassment stuff. Just chat with her and maybe tell her you and some other work buddies are going to bar after work. Then ask if she'd like to join you. If she says no, then no big deal. But be very careful. If you start to date her and then break up, it's going to get hairy. Be prepared to feel awkward.

The point is to get it done and get on with your life. If she says no, there are better women out there for you. Move on. Don't fixate on it. Be gracious in defeat. Remember: Each woman is totally different. Once you've got one figured out, another one will throw you a curve ball.

So did you ask her out? Did she turn you down? Well, so what? You gave it a try. I'm betting even if she did turn you down, she's thinking of you and you might just get lucky enough and she'll ask you out in a few weeks. This is why it's so important to handle rejection graciously. If you get too upset, she's going to think you're weird and be glad she turned you down. But if you take it in stride, she's going to want to know what's up with you.

WHAT WE LEARNED:
- The woman you have a crush on may like you.
- Start a dialogue with her by saying "hi" when you see her.
- Always smile and act friendly.
- Be confident in your approach when you ask her out. (Already have a plan of what you want to do—dinner and a movie, etc.)
- If she turns you down, move on. Never be a sore loser.

HOW TO TALK TO A WOMAN

After you've got the signal, which we talked about earlier, it's time to walk right up to this girl and get things going. It is so important to know how to start that initial conversation. Without the conversation, there can be no "getting to know you" date. And we all know that there is no simple way to ask a woman out. There is no magical potion to make it any easier. The thing is, she's either going to say yes or she's going to say no.

You may not believe this, but when women are asked what really works when a man is trying to pick them up, most will say, "He smiled at me." Never underestimate the power of a smile! Of course, a lecherous grin isn't going to cut it. But a nice smile should work wonders with anyone. A smile disarms even the biggest bitch on the planet. That's why earlier in the book I said that it is important for your teeth to look their best.

So how do you do it? How do you start that initial conversation? Simple. Walk up to her, smile and say, "Hi." Wait for her to respond and after she does, introduce yourself. And then…*Get her to talk about herself.* If you can get her talking about herself, all you're going to have to do is nod every so often. Asking questions about her work or where she went to school or whatever is a good way to get her talking. Women love to talk and when it's about them, be prepared to be there all night.

WHEN TALKING, YOU SHOULD:
- Never contradict her.
- Never roll your eyes.
- Never touch her unless she's touched you first. Not even to get an eyelash off her face. Just tell her she's got one and if she leans in for you to get it, get it. But not unless invited.
- Remember her name and put it into the conversation, "So, Jane, how long have you lived here?"
- Never stare at other chicks while talking to her.
- Never look distracted or bored, even if you are.

It is important to understand that once you have her talking, you have an opportunity to date her. Don't blow it. Use the guidelines for talking from the examples I've provided. This should work every time. If it doesn't, you're doing something wrong or you're trying too hard. Don't try too hard and don't act desperate. Don't give her a reason to say no.

A FEW ICEBREAKERS:
- "Do you have the time?" (If you have a watch on, don't use this one, unless it's broken.)
- Compliment her on something, like her watch or earrings.
- "Hi, how are you?"

Asking any open-ended question will spur her attention. This will get her talking and the rest should take care of itself. There is no science or mystery to it. It's all about making a little connection with someone for a period of time. Doing it this way ensures that you won't have much embarrassment and she won't call you a loser. If she does, she's a royal bitch and you're better off without her.

Remember that if she's not talking much or looking around anxiously, this doesn't mean she doesn't want to talk. She could be very nervous. *She* could be shy. Watch for the signs. See if she's interested in you. If she is, she'll let you know.

After you've talked for a while, decide if you want to get her phone number. If you do...

SAY THIS:
- "I really have to get going, but I'd love to talk to you some more. Can I get your number? Maybe we could go out sometime."

When you ask for it, ask for it with confidence, as if you don't expect her to turn you down. Also, don't stumble over your words so you'll have to repeat yourself. The thing is, it's not that hard to talk to a woman. And talk to her as if you're just shooting the breeze. Never let her in on the fact that you're *that* interested. But, of course, if you're talking to her, she probably already knows you're interested.

A FEW MORE GUIDELINES:
- Never try to outsmart a woman.
- Never smother her with too many compliments or too much attention.
- Never touch her unless invited.

- Never use lame pick-up lines.
- Never disrespect her.
- Never approach a woman who's wearing a scowl.

SOME PLACES YOU CAN PICK HER UP:
- Parties.
- Bars.
- Clubs.
- Restaurants.
- Grocery stores.
- Video stores.
- Bookstores.
- The post office.
- The train station.
- Just about anywhere in public.

You always need some of your buddies to go with you when you're out at clubs or parties. Never stand alone by yourself. This looks creepy and you'll be known as that guy "alone in the corner drinking himself into oblivion." Never, ever drink too much. Keep yourself in check as no chick likes a horny, drunken fool.

WHAT WE LEARNED:
- Approach a woman with a smile and a "Hi."
- Introduce yourself.
- Get her to talk about herself.
- Ask open-ended questions.

REHEARSAL FOR TALKING TO CHICKS

Let's get right to the point and the point of this chapter is rehearsing for talking to chicks. It is comprised of pretend dialogue. You don't have to use it verbatim or even use it; this is just to let you know how it usually goes. It might also be a good idea to practice with yourself—or a friend—in front of a mirror. Don't feel like a fool, either. It's important to make the mistakes *before* you go out. The key is to be prepared. The more you do this, the better you will get at it and soon it will be second nature.

That's your goal. Expect to strike out a few times before you get a hit.

Also, don't create a script to follow. If she says something you didn't expect and you don't have an answer, you'll end up getting tongue-tied. Be willing to be flexible.

And, as always, before you approach her, make a little eye contact. Meet her eyes a few times before you proceed. If she's not meeting your gaze at all, proceed with caution or don't proceed at all. Remember to wait for the signal to step to it. And if you're getting it, you'll know it.

WHAT ARE THE SIGNALS?
- She will throw you a smile.
- She will give you a shy or coy look.
- She will look a little nervous, as if you caught her staring at you.

The key is to *not* stare at her. Casually glance over. Watch her for a few moments and try to catch her gaze. Once you do, give her a smile, wait a few seconds for her to respond and then immediately look away and start talking with one of your friends. This is what I like to call the "whatever" approach. Whatever happens is fine. If she likes you, whatever. If she doesn't, whatever. You're just there to be sociable, just like her. Remember it's all in the attitude. You're just a friendly, good-natured guy. But you're also confident enough to know that you have the ability to talk to a woman.

Okay. Let's say you're sitting at the bar and a hot chick sits down near you. Wait a few minutes and then glance in her direction and say—loudly enough for her to hear you—"Hi."

"Hi," she says.

"I know this is stupid," you say. "But I heard this really great pick-up line the other day. Wanna hear it?"

Screech! You say, *But you told me not to ever use pick-up lines!* Okay, you're not using a pick-up line here to actually pick her up. You're using a pick-up line to start a conversation. Doing it this way will disarm her. Try it and see. This is more like a joke than a pick-up line, okay? (Also, if you can't handle doing it as a joke, don't use it. Just ask if she'd like a drink or something.)

"Sure," she says.

"I'm one and you're one, let's get together and make two," you say and laugh. "How bad is that?"

"It's terrible," she says and laughs.

"I know," you say. "I didn't offend you, did I?"

"No, I'm a big girl," she says. "I can take it."

"So," you say. "Tell me a little about yourself. Where do you work?"

This allows her to talk about herself. Once you do this, it's in her court. Just continue to interject other little questions as she's talking. *This* is the key to talking to women. They love to yammer about themselves. Get them talking about themselves and you've got it made. And you do this by asking them questions.

QUESTIONS LIKE:
- Where do you work?
- Do you enjoy your job?
- Where did you go to school?
- What was your major?
- Did you see that movie?

After she's talked for a while, tell her you have to get going, but you'd love to continue the conversation, maybe over dinner sometime. And ask for her number. And you're done. Remember, you should exude confidence at all times, even if she rejects you. Take it like a man and say, "Oh, that's cool," if she turns your down and give her a smile before you leave. Yes, it might sting a little, but if you can do this, you will get her thinking about you.

On the other hand, if she's interested in you, she will want to go out on a date. And if she's not interested, then you're back in the game again. Repeat this and surely you will have success of some kind. The important thing to keep in mind is that the first few times you do this, expect to strike out. You're honing your craft and it will take several attempts to get it right. Don't be afraid to make mistakes and don't be afraid to try again. Tell yourself you have to do this exercise and soon it will come as second nature.

As you do this, remember: It's okay to be a little nervous. You're human, aren't you? It's okay if you embarrass yourself a few times. Once you get over your initial hesitation, it will get easier and easier. If you do embarrass yourself, laugh it off. Women expect a little humility because it means you're not going to expect too much of them and that helps take the pressure off.

Remember the most important thing to know is that women have to give you the signal to approach. Once you get it, approach with confidence. But you will first have to let them know you're a little interested and you do that by giving her a smile or a "Hello."

One last thing. Once you meet a woman, you will probably shake her hand after you've introduced yourself. Give her a nice handshake and then withdraw your hand. Never let it linger. Women hate bad handshakes. Remember, women are always tying to protect their personal space so it's best you don't get too close. Also, don't kiss her hand or cheek or try to give her a hug. I've seen this on a lot of TV reality shows and it just looks creepy. So, it's not a good idea to do this in real life, unless you're willing to take the chance of getting slapped.

That should give you plenty to chew on for a while. The key is always confidence. Have confidence and everything else should fall into place. Using these methods should get you in the door.

WHAT WE LEARNED:
- Talking to a woman isn't that hard. Just act like she's any other normal human being.
- Don't be afraid to strike out a few times.
- Starting a conversation is the first step to picking her up.
- Always smile and act nice, but be confident.
- If she turns you down, be gracious and move on.

KIDS

There may be a possibility that the woman of your dreams has a kid or two. For some men, this is not a big deal. However, I have never understood why this freaks other men out. At least you know she's fertile. For some reason guys think because she's got a kid or two she's damaged goods.

That is the way a jerk thinks. What should it matter? Apparently her first relationship didn't work out. This doesn't mean that if you get into a relationship with her that it's doomed from the get-go. If she has a kid—or kids—grow up. I know that a lot of guys don't want an Instant Family and that's fine. I also know a lot of super-hot chicks who have kids and don't date much because of it. (And I mean *super*-hot.)

So, just find out before you take her out if she's got any kids. If she's got a few, just smile and move away from her if it makes you that uncomfortable. But don't treat her like she's got the plague.

One more note. Just because she's got kids doesn't mean she's easy. Always be kind and respectful. That's building good Karma and we could all use some good Karma.

WHAT WE LEARNED:
- Some women already have kids. If you don't want to deal with that, be upfront about it. Never waste her time.

DON'T TRY TO IMPRESS HER

I can just hear you asking, *What? Don't try to impress her? What's this?* Calm down and sit back and listen.

Yes, you're going to impress her by doing stuff like cleaning your home and getting some new threads. But if *you* go out of your way to tell her how great you are, she's just going to think you're either a liar or an egomaniac. Never, ever try to convince anyone of your greatness. They will either see it or not. Never, ever be too obvious. Obvious=desperate and a chick can see right through that.

Remember, the first few dates are reserved for her. Make her feel special. Let her talk your ear off. Be considerate to her and keep your distance. If she wants you, she will let you know.

DO LITTLE THINGS THAT SPEAK FOR THEMSELVES:
- Open doors.
- Unlock her side of the car first.
- Pay the check.
- And all that other stuff I've told you about.

AVOID TALKING:
- About yourself. You're there to get to know her.
- About how great you are.

- About your conquests—real or otherwise.
- About your poetry and at all costs, please do not ask her to read it until after you've sealed the deal.

When she says, "Tell me about yourself," tell her about yourself. Tell her where you went to school and where you live and work and all that. She's asking this so she can tell what kind of guy you are. Let her know upfront about your work and all that. Talk about yourself, but always stop every once in a while and ask her a question like, "Where did *you* grow up?" and stuff like that. Treat her as if she were any other "normal" person you want to get to know better.

And that's all you're doing here. Sure, you might want to be her boyfriend, but this time is reserved to get to know her. Use this time to just *be.* Stop worrying about your aspirations for a few minutes and engage in a conversation with another human being. Also, stop worrying about after the date and stop thinking about what color her panties are. Don't ever expect more than what you have in the moment. If you get it, great. If not, why worry complain about it? This is called dating, after all. This is her time and treat it as such. Being respectful is going to get you major points. Pushing yourself on her and trying to get into pants will get you the cold shoulder.

Important note: Touchy, feely, kissy is really creepy. Even if you are from a family that does this, try to control yourself. Women don't like these kinds of guys. Keep your hands to yourself. She will give you the signal to touch her and it will be subtle—a nod of the head, a look into the eyes, chin in the air as she stares into your eyes. Just don't get familiar too soon.

In the same vein, desperation/egomania speaks for itself. Don't tell her how many women you've slept with in order to impress her. More than likely it will just piss her off and if she asks, just shrug and ask her the exact same question. Say that you prefer not to kiss and tell. She *will* change the subject. Neither one of you need to know that anyway because no matter how many it was, it's always *too* many. Reserve this fight for when you've been going out for a while. (And once you get to it, I feel for both of you.)

WHAT WE LEARNED:

- Don't try to impress her by telling her how great you are.
- Avoid talking—or over-talking—about yourself. Just give her a little something to go on. If she wants to know, she'll ask.
- Never brag.
- Remember, at first, this is all about her. Get to know her.

BAD SIGNS

Just so you will know, there are women out there who will try and take advantage of you and your good nature. Be cautious with a hot chick if she asks to borrow money, credit cards, etc. If she steals your stuff, dump her. You could ask why she did it but she's just going to act like she doesn't know what you're talking about.

There are women out there who will use you. Believe me, there are. If you're not getting anything out of it, why bother? And if you are getting something out of it and don't mind, then that is your business, mister. I'm just giving you a head's up on this one.

WHAT WE LEARNED:

- Some chicks are out to use you.
- Be cautious if she starts asking for money, etc.

THE WAY A WOMAN FLIRTS

A woman can flirt in various ways and if you know what signs to look for, you can ascertain if she likes you or not. Wanna find out if she's really interested? Here's how. And this is universal; it has been going on forever. It won't change tomorrow.

WHEN A WOMAN SEES SOMEONE SHE'S INTERESTED IN:

- She will smile.
- She will lift her eyebrows.
- She will open her eyes wide to gaze at them.
- She will tilt her head to the side.
- She will look away, almost in embarrassment.
- She might giggle nervously and hide her face in her hands.
- She will toss or play with her hair.
- She will raise her shoulders.

- She may mirror his actions, like look at her watch after he looks at his.
- And, more than likely, she will get tongue-tied. As I've said, she's just as nervous as you are. Keep that in mind and give her a break if she's acting strange.

If she does any of these things in any order or at any time, this means she's interested in you. If you don't get any of these signals, it's probably a sign she's not interested.

WHAT WE LEARNED:
- Watch for the signs to see if she digs you. If you ain't getting any, she ain't getting you.

YOU CAN'T DANCE

Well, maybe you can. But it should be contained behind closed doors unless you're a professional.

Okay, say you're at a club and this really hot chick pulls you to the dance floor. Now what the hell are you supposed to do? Listen. Don't bust a groove. Let her dance around you. Don't shake your butt out there or do your famous break-dancing moves. Don't raise the roof. Don't do the cabbage patch. Just let her groove around you and keep your eyes on her. Hopefully, it will be over very soon.

A woman always leads on the dance floor—unless it's ballroom dancing—or you just end up looking like a fool. Follow her movements if she's gotten you out there. That way, you look like you're just interested in her but you don't end up looking like a dork. Don't stand still but do move a little, but not too much as you'll end up looking like you're either gay or a dancing fool.

WHAT WE LEARNED:
- You can't dance. If you can, keep it to yourself.
- If she makes you dance, don't stand still. Just follow her movements but don't overdo it.

MAKE HER LAUGH—BUT DON'T TRY TO BE FUNNY

Contradiction? Hardly. If you can make her laugh, she's gonna stick around a little while to see what else you can do. But *try* to make her laugh and all you're gonna hear is crickets. So, therefore, no corny jokes and if you have to say something funny and witty, save it. It will always come out wrong. Don't act too funny. Most people are not natural comedians. If you're one of the lucky few, go for it. But only if you get regular laughs from those close to you.

Another lovely lady I know said this, "This guy, bless his heart, this guy was so un-funny it was almost funny. He told these corny jokes and whenever there was an opening for him to say something 'funny,' he would. I might have given him a chance but he really got on my nerves. It was one of the longest dates I've ever been on."

Don't be this guy. You could end up in a dating book!

If you want her to laugh, why not learn a few—clean!—jokes. (Dirty jokes are a real turn-off.) Self-deprecating humor is always good, too. But be natural. If you can't tell a good joke, then don't. As your nervousness wanes, say something a little funny. But never overdo it. Never get on her nerves. Never try to make her laugh. If you do this, she will laugh at you—behind your back. And that will suck.

WHAT WE LEARNED:
- Don't try too hard to make her laugh.
- A little self-deprecating humor can be good in small doses.

WOMEN ARE THE WORLD'S MYSTERY

I admit it. Women are hard to figure out. What works for one will never work with another. But we all have basic needs and desires. We all want a good man. Be a good man and you will find yourself a good woman.

SOME THINGS THAT WOMEN REALLY LIKE:

- Compliments. Compliment her dress or her jewelry or anything. She spent a long time getting ready, after all. She'll be glad someone noticed.
- Chocolate.
- New shoes.
- A man who is good in bed.
- A man who pays for dinner.
- A man who can work on her car.
- A man who listens to her.
- Planning her dream wedding.
- Jewelry.
- Men.

YOU'VE GOT HER NUMBER, NOW WHAT?

Call her! I mean, what else are you gonna do with it? Are you gonna play the stupid waiting game? You know which one I'm talking about. It's where you get a chick's phone number and wait two, three, four days to call her. Don't! If you do this, it means that you're a game player. You asked for that number, now summon your courage and call her already. *Man,* you say, *this seems harder than getting her number in the first place.* That's because you still fear rejection. Well, you'll never know until you try and you asked for that number for a reason. For all you know, she's waiting on you to call. She wants you to call. And if she doesn't, she won't pick up.

Remember, if she didn't want you to call, she wouldn't have given you her number. If she gave you a fake number, then she's just a bitch. It's that simple.

So, wait until the next day. Maybe in the evening sometime when you know she'll answer. Say, hello, hi, this is—whatever your name is—we met at—wherever you met—and let it go from there. Don't be afraid. She's a person just like you.

So, you've got her on the phone. Now what? Be yourself. That should be easy enough. Talk to her for a little while, asking about her day and her work and all that. Then, ask her out for a date. You should always have a plan, by the way. Whether you want to take her for a nice dinner or to a concert or wherever. *You make the plans.* Women hate it when guys don't know where to go. Never say, "We'll go where you want to." No, no, no! Say, "I thought we could try this new restaurant. How about it?" Or, "I know this nice little restaurant…"

If you call her and she doesn't answer, leave a very short, brief message. Say something like, "This is Bob. We met at the bookstore. Anyway, just wanted to call and see what's going on. My number is 867-5309. Thanks."

And don't hesitate. Say it like you mean it. Say it like a man. Just say it, for God's sake! And let her call you back. If she doesn't, she's not interested and you just saved yourself some embarrassment and time. Make sure you don't grovel by calling her back several times. If you think something got screwed up with the message, wait until the next day and give it another try. If you still don't hear from her, it's because she doesn't want to talk to you.

Now, if and when she returns your message, make sure she remembers you by saying something like, "Yeah, hello. I met you at the grocery store?"

She says, "Yeah, I know who you are."

And then ask her how it's going. Again—important note here—let her talk! Ask about her day and her job and her cat. Of course, she should ask you about yourself, too, and when she does, give short, nice answers.

And blah, blah, blah.

Once you've let her talk for a few minutes, step in and ask her out. You should already know where you want to take her. Whether it's to dinner, for drinks or to see some band. Ask her, let her answer and there you go. It's done.

You're getting good at this, aren't you?

WHAT WE LEARNED:
- Once you get her number, call her the next day.
- Be sure to ask her out on a date once you've got her on the phone.
- Have a plan of where you want to take her.

IF YOU HOUND HER...

You've just taken her out and had a nice time. The night is ending and you're at her front door. You spent some money and now you want something back for it. You try to push yourself on your date.

You are headed for trouble.

First of all, just because you spent a little money doesn't mean that you're going to get some. You can never make assumptions about a woman. As soon as you do, she will turn on a dime and do the exact opposite of what you think she will do. You think that if you "work" her a little, you can have sex. Or, rather, you're entitled to have sex.

Nope.

Let's just say this: Don't work her to get laid. If she wants to have sex with you, she will let you know. Don't try to guilt her into it. And don't try to pull any stupid rules on her either, like no kissing on the first date or whatever. Remember, it is up to her and her alone if you two have sex. I don't care how much dinner cost or how much trouble you went to. It will happen when and if she says it will happen. And if it doesn't, be courteous, tell her you had a wonderful time, and go home.

WHAT WE LEARNED:
- Never assume a woman is going to give it up just because you bought her dinner.
- Don't "work" her in order to get some.

STALKER MATERIAL? DON'T BE!

Have you met the girl of your dreams and she turned you down? Or did you take her on a date or two and now she's not returning your calls? Now you can't get her out your head, can you? You turned into a stalker and...well, stalked her.

First of all, this is illegal and extremely creepy. This is the kind of stuff that will mess your life up for good.

IF YOU FIND THAT YOU...
- Stand outside her apartment.
- Wait outside her work.

- Call her and then hang up.
- "Find" yourself being in the same place as her a lot.

…then you are stalker material. Don't be! Stop this behavior right now. If she doesn't like you, there's nothing you can do about it. She isn't going to come around. Leave her alone. Go find another chick to love on.

If you find yourself obsessing about one particular girl, find a way to get her out of your system. Maybe she's a girl that you've had a crush on and never had the courage to talk to. Maybe you had one date or shared a drink but she doesn't want anything to do with you now. *Take the hint!* Find a new girl and see if she works out or, failing that, find a new hobby or work on your poetry. Anything you can do to get her out of your mind, do it.

You lament, *But it was meant to be!* No it wasn't. if she doesn't want you, forget her. Don't let this obsessive train of thoughts get you into some major trouble. This chick could have a mean older brother or an ex-boyfriend who's a wrestler. She could have your butt kicked three ways to Sunday. She could also have you arrested.

Remember, love does sometimes hurt. But it does get better. Get over this one girl and move on with your life.

WHAT WE LEARNED:
- If you stalk her, you just might go to jail and become someone's bitch.

IS SHE STALKER MATERIAL?

Yes, as unlikely as it may seem, there are women out there who might become obsessed with you. You may find that she's showing up at your work or leaving weird messages on your machine. If so, you've got yourself a stalker.

When and if this happens, it's going to be hard to rationalize with her. You can try and have a talk, but be very forward and let her know that the relationship has ended. But understand that, more than likely, she will wig out, cry and act just plain weird. Best to nip this in the bud to begin with. If you get any weird *Fatal Attraction* vibes, call it an early night and go home.

Another thing about women is that they can get insulted at the smallest things. Maybe you forgot to tell her how nice she looks or whatever then, before you know it, she's throwing a fit. When this happens, apologize and smile, let her rant and rave and then change the topic of conversation. She should get the hint and apologize. This chick is probably not crazy but just a little hotheaded, as most women are. Be prepared for that. But if she won't let it go, she's probably not just a little hotheaded and more like a little crazy. If so, maybe break it off with her.

WHAT WE LEARNED:
- Some chicks might be stalker material.
- It's best to leave these chicks alone.
- Women can and will get insulted at the smallest things. Learn to deal with it.

CHICK FLICKS

Yes, you can. Endure them. Be a man. Be strong. And take her to see that damn movie. You can nap through it if you like. If she asks what you think, say, "It was good. What did *you* think?"

See what you're doing here? Yeah, you're getting smarter.

FIRST DATE—FIRST NERVOUS BREAKDOWN

Before I say anything else, let me say this: Going out with a woman for the first time is very similar to going on a job interview. You have to be relaxed but be aware that you're trying to make the best impression. Don't do anything on a first date that you wouldn't on a job interview. Act sociable but never overbearing or too eager.

A girl I know told me this, "The first date is always the worse. I don't know why, maybe it's because we don't know each other and there is always expectation and tension. But if the guy's cool and nice and he pays for dinner and keeps his hands to himself, then I might consider going on a second date. I hate to admit it, but if he does anything on that first date that I don't like, there *is* no second date after that."

HOW TO GET A GIRLFRIEND

Harsh reality there. But very insightful. The point is, if you like this chick, do everything in your power to get that second date and, hopefully, a third. After the third date, more than likely, you're gonna get to see her boobies.

First of all, bring her a little something that lets her know you appreciate her taking the time to go out with you, but not something corny like a teddy bear.

THINGS THAT YOU CAN GIVE HER:

- A bouquet of flowers—daisies, lilies, etc. but not a rose. (Roses are serious and you want this to be fun. You can send her roses later on.)
- A small box of good chocolates. (Godiva for instance.)

The most important thing on a first date is to let her take the lead. Sit back, relax and enjoy the evening. Ask her about herself. She loves to talk, after all. (If you haven't learned anything by now, you should have learned that.) Ask her about her job, her family, her friends, her doll collection, what movies she likes. There is a plethora of information stored inside her head and all you have to do is ask. But don't interrogate her—just allow her the opportunity to talk by carrying on a conversation as you would with anyone else.

If she's shy and doesn't talk much, maybe suggest a movie. Afterwards, she might come out of her shell. It'll give you something to talk about. Shy girls are tough. You can never tell what's going on inside their noggins. Good luck with those ones.

On your first date, you should make all the arrangements. You should pick her up right on time. (Never early and most certainly never late.) You know she won't be ready and while she's finishing up, look around her place and find out what kind of girl she is. Does she have a roommate? A cat? Why does she have so many pillows on the couch? And what's with all the candles?

Once she appears, she is going to want a compliment from you because she just spent a long time getting ready and she changed five times before settling on this outfit.

Take a few seconds to take her in. She does look mighty fine! Don't hesitate to tell her how nice she looks. Don't just say, "You look good." Say, "Wow, you look great!" But, on the other hand, don't gush! A nice, simple compliment will do and she will appreciate this.

Once in the car, if you're nervous and can't think of anything to say, say, "I just got this CD. Do you like Sinatra?"

Turn it on but keep the speakers low. You don't want to have to yell over the music to be heard. This will take the pressure off and help both of you to relax.

Remember, she's just as nervous as you, if not more so. Be considerate and nice and keep your distance so she'll begin to trust you. Building trust with a lady is a big thing. Do that and you're in.

Now it's time for you to take charge. Tell her what you've got planned for the evening as you're driving to your destination. Smile and ask her about her day. Let her do the talking and act like you're very interested in what she has to say and just not in what she has under that dress.

Of course, you are going to take her to a nice restaurant. Pull up and, if it has valet parking, go for it. This will impress her. (It impresses me, anyway.)

Once inside the restaurant, you know to pull her chair out for her and to let her sit first, right? I knew you did. Good boy. Now, sit down and have a nice meal. And as you're enjoying your meal, start looking for the signs.

THERE ARE INNUMERABLE WAYS TO TELL IF SHE LIKES YOU:

- Is she touching your arm? Holding your gaze?
- Is she laughing at your little jokes?
- Is she asking questions about your life?

Women think that all you want is to get laid. Sure, she's right to a certain degree, isn't she? However, you have to show her you *want* to know her first. All that good sex can come later. Show her that you're willing to take the time to get to know her.

Have a good time and when you take her home, give her a peck on her cheek at the door, if she offers it to you. If not, date's over and so is your impending relationship. Always wait until the end of the date to make a move. Don't try to hold her hand. Even this small gesture is a signal to her that you're moving too fast.

She might just ask you inside for a cup of coffee. If so, go for it. But don't think that just because she's asking you in that you're going to get laid. Just think that it's for a cup of coffee. Never assume anything. If she wants you, let her come to you. Don't jump *her* bones. Let her make the first move. Watch for signs. If she's touching your arm and smiling or leaning over in a way so you can catch a glimpse of her luscious breasts, she probably wants it. If not, she just wants to talk some more, you poor thing.

A FEW IMPORTANT THINGS TO NEVER DO ON DATES:

- Don't do drugs. They can make you impotent. They're also illegal.
- Don't drink too much. This will make you stupid and impotent as well.
- Don't just stare at her cleavage all night. Look into her eyes a few times.
- If you spill something, just laugh it off. Don't freak out over it.

Now you've got the first one done. *Phew.* Aren't you glad that's over? What about the next one? Just before you leave, ask her, "Would you like to do this again?" If you've played your cards right, she should reply in the affirmative. If not, she should tell you no. If yes, tell her that you'll call her and thank her for a lovely evening.

On your next date, do something creative. Do something fun and special. And always plan it from start to finish. Just because she's in control, doesn't mean you can't take charge or that you shouldn't. (At least when it comes to making the arrangements.)

Important tip every man should know: Never expect sex or even a kiss on the first date. Even some girls who are absolute freaks won't kiss on the first date. Be a gentleman. Be nice. Keep your hands to yourself and your pants zipped. If she unzips them… Hey, let her do what she has to do.

WHAT WE LEARNED:

- Treat your first date as you would a job interview.
- Be a gentleman the entire time by opening her car door first, pulling out her chair, etc.

- Bring her a small, nice gift that's not too tacky.
- Let her do most of the talking but don't interrogate her.

YOUR FIRST KISS

The first kiss is so very important and so very sweet. It's the first time your lips meet hers and the only time you are going to get to prove yourself. Do it right the first time and she will be coming back for more.

But first, you need the signal from her that it's okay. You'll know when it's cool where there's usually a moment of silence and then a connection with the eyes.

After you've gotten the signal, initiate that first kiss. Do it slowly, but like it's the only thing on your mind. Like there is nothing in the world you'd rather be doing. Look at her like there's no one else around—if you're lucky, there won't be—and don't ask if you can do it. Just look her right in the eye, bend down and pull her to you. She will swoon. I don't know what it is about having a guy pull you to him that is so sexy, but just know it is.

Once your mouth is on top of hers, there are two ways to go about it. One is to give her a nice, soft mouth kiss with no tongue. Just pucker up and press your lips against hers softly and then pull back. See if she wants another. If her eyes are still closed, she does. The other is to give her a gut-wrenching, weak in the knees kiss.

And let nature take its course.

Once you're done with that first kiss, pull back and stare her directly in the eyes. If she hasn't asked you in, tell her, "I had a great time tonight. I hope we can do it again." And if you gave her a good kiss, you will.

WHAT WE LEARNED:
- No slobbering, tongue kisses.
- Something nice and soft at first.

SAFE SEX

If you get lucky, be safe and *always* insist on a condom. You know that a woman can get pregnant, don't you? And you know how that works, right? If not, go ask your mother about it and she'll set you straight.

Also, diseases. You know that you can contract certain disease from sex, right? Yeah, like the clap and all kinds of icky stuff. If you have no clue as to what I'm talking about, go look it up on the internet. There's a whole world of information just waiting for you.

Be informed. Be smart. Be safe.

WHAT TO DO IN THE BEDROOM

It might be a good thing to know that women are hard-wired for sex just like you. Take a minute to get your head around that. Yes, women want it just as much as men. Believe it or not, women love sex. I can attest to this. I know a woman in her sixties who talks of nothing else. Don't get grossed out, this only validates what I'm saying.

The #1 rule you must accept: Woman are in control. *Flip side:* She wants you to take it—in the bedroom. But don't be too aggressive at first. Never jump the gun—or her bones—until she's given you the greenlight. Just a touch to let her know you're not a sissy. Be subtle. Most women—generalizing here—want a man to dominate them once they're between the sheets. She *wants* you to rock her world. Give her something memorable and she'll come back for more. And if she never wants to see you again, she will definitely keep your number around when she needs some sex.

Before any of this can happen, you need to get yourself prepared to give her an evening of sensual delights. Read sexy erotica. Women usually write erotica, so if you're thinking Henry Miller, don't. Women erotica writers know what turns women on and they put it (sometimes explicitly) in their books. Note: Don't take BDSM literally unless she asks—and she might. Bringing in a pair of handcuffs or some rope will scare the crap out of her. Now if she does it to you, hang on for the ride. There are many, many kinky girls out there. They can't wait to get their hands on you.

So, once you get to the sex, just let nature take its course. But be aware of the body you're groping. You have to understand that there aren't just two parts of a woman—her vagina and her boobs. There are various gateways—places that often don't get touched but bring out the lust—to her sexuality

A WOMAN'S GATEWAYS:
- Her neck. (Always use a flat tongue as you kiss/suck at her neck.)
- The small of her back. (Kiss it, lick it, worship it.)
- Her inner thighs. (Umm…just a light finger touch.)
- The back of the knees. (Kiss them lightly.)

Be sure to pay attention to these. If you do, you'll have her swooning. And that means she'll come back for more.

WHAT WE LEARNED:
- Be sure to use a condom.
- Read some erotica written by women.
- Take charge of the sex. Be the man in the bedroom.
- Women like sex just as much as men.
- Take care with a woman's gateways.

BEAUTIFUL WOMEN ABROAD

Just something to consider. Another good way to meet some lovely ladies is to travel. Women who reside in other countries will find you more appealing than their native man. It's the English accent principal. Over here, it sounds charming. Over there, it sounds ordinary. You, being a foreigner to her native land, could stand a good chance of hooking up because you're not from around there.

Once you meet a lovely girl, ask her to show you around the city if she has time. Or ask her if she'd like a drink. And let it go from there. The same rules apply.

ONCE YOU'VE GOT HER, HERE'S HOW TO KEEP HER

These next few chapters are going to concentrate on how to keep your new girl once you've found her. Listen carefully and you could very well have the love of your life eating from the palm of your hand. Having a girl you can call your own is like nothing else. No more lonely Saturday nights. No more whining about never getting laid. You're getting laid all the time now because you and she are, as they say, pair bonding. Dare I say it? You and she are…*falling in love.*

Now what? How do you even begin to understand her inner workings? If you thought trying to date was hard, this might be a little tougher. Because now she isn't always acting like she did on the first few dates. And she wants to do this thing called "talking."

Oh, boy. We've got more work to do. Let's step to it.

THE BITCH IS BACK: DEALING WITH PMS

If you've been dating her for a while, there will come a day when your woman acts a little…*off.* She might act crazy, be bitchier than normal and not respond to your lecherous advances. This little hell is fondly known as PMS and that's when her hormones have been kicked into overdrive. She's just finished ovulating and that damned egg is about to drop but before it does, she must endure torment and despair for a few days.

Most men don't have a clue as to what PMS is all about. And, let's be honest, you really don't *want* to know anything about it, do you? Well, tough. You've got a girlfriend now and this is information that might save you some future pain.

Let me tell you what it's like. It's like the whole world is pissing you off and you feel as though you could bite a ten-penny nail in half. Nothing makes sense and everything is annoying. Your breasts are so sore you can't even touch them. And then you get zits and you gain five pounds for no reason. Your belly swells and, on top of that, you can't get enough chocolate or salty foods. It's like you're walking around with a perpetual black cloud hanging over your head and there's nothing you can do about it.

So, you cry and cry and then feel stupid about it all. After it's over, you hope no one got hurt. Body count, please?

Sounds fun, doesn't it? You try being a woman for one day and you'll be thankful for us in ways you could never imagine.

The best thing you can do: Give her some space. Back off her for a few days. Tell her to call you when she wants to talk. Expect her to pick fights with you. Her hormones are going insane right now and she is not herself. Anything *can* and *will* set her off, especially if you leave socks lying around.

HOW TO TELL IF SHE'S PMSING—well, there shouldn't be any doubt, but if there is:
- She's snappy.
- Her belly swells.
- She may get a few zits.
- She just told you she hates your guts and all you did was ask her if she wanted a foot rub.

Don't take it personally. She's not herself right now. Forgive her and move on. And no, you can't touch her boobies right now. They are tender and sore as all get out and that's why she's grumpy. You'd be grumpy, too.

This doesn't necessarily mean she is going to try to make your life a living hell, but if you do something to get on her nerves— like heavy breathing—she might. Just stay your distance, ask *once* if anything is wrong and know she'll snap out of it in a few days. Be forgiving of anything bitchy she says during this time. She doesn't mean it, okay? I know it hurts, but she'll make it up to you later.

Now let's touch on the other subject: Her period. Do not put this book down and run away! You should know what this is all about and if you don't, take a class or something. But, more importantly, don't make her feel weird because of it. It's natural. (And you'll probably be happy when it comes every month—that means she's not knocked up!) All women have to have to deal with it each and every month. No wonder we're almost crazy.

Do her a favor and keep a bottle of ibuprofen around for her cramps. And some ice cream. And ask if she would like a foot rub and then give her the best foot rub around. Be gentle and kind with her while all this is going on and if you are, you'll never get rid of her. She's not going to let a good guy like you get away.

Also, ask her if there's anything she wants you to do for her. Like buying her groceries. Or watering her plants. Or helping her around the house. And if she wants you to pick up some tampons, do it. Everyone knows they're not for you.

Chances are, she won't want to have sex once she's on the rag but if she does, just put a towel down. (Women do sometimes get horny during this time of the month.) Women don't bleed quarts and quarts of blood but it can get a little messy. And don't get grossed out about it, either. It's hard enough on us without having you go, "Ick!"

But the most important thing you can do is be understanding of her monthly curse and just try to ignore her screaming at you about the toilet seat. (Which should *always* be left down.)

WHAT WE LEARNED:
- PMS is a living hell. Chances are, when she has it, your life will be a living hell as well.
- Don't make her feel bad about her period.
- Be nice and considerate during these times.
- Stay out of her way.
- If she bites your head off, know it's the hormones talking. She'll be back to herself in a few days.

MYSTERY DATE

After you've been seeing your girl for a while, you might want to spice things up. (A little while is a few months, not a few weeks.) One good way to make her squeal like a little girl is to schedule a Mystery Date.

All women go ga-ga over this stuff. It's like, "He cares so much, he told me we were going to have a Mystery Date." What's in it for you? Just a night of hot, intense sex is all. You game?

You will schedule the Mystery Date but, of course, you won't tell her anything about it. Just ask her out for the night and tell her you are going on a Mystery Date. If she asks what you're talking about, just say, "It's a mystery, baby. If I told you, it wouldn't be a mystery, would it?"

Okay, here's how to do it. First of all, figure out how much cash you have to spend. Next, see what your city has to offer. If there's nothing much you can schedule, like a tour of the aquarium after hours, maybe buy a couple of tickets to Vegas and get a nice suite with champagne on ice when you arrive. If you can do a limo, then you are going to be the man!

If Vegas is out of the question and you don't have much cash, look around at your other options. Does your city have a riverboat? You can do any attractions that neither of you have been to since you were little kids. Or take her to a theme park. Anything that would surprise her and isn't the standard "dinner and a movie." You could also get a fancy hotel suite with a Jacuzzi. Just be sure to go get the key before you take her there.

Mystery Dates are good for anniversaries or if you feel her attention is waning a little. They're also good anytime, but especially at the first of a relationship. Do stuff like this and you'll never get rid of her. You have been warned.

WHAT WE LEARNED:

- Organize a mystery date and you will have the happiest girl in the world.

SEDUCTION 101

Obviously, this isn't first date kind of stuff. Once you've been seeing a girl for a while—and have already gotten the preliminary sex over—give her a special night. Women love romance even though most guys just don't get it. We've been fed this stuff from movies and TV since we were little girls and it's not going to change anytime soon. We want our man to cater to us occasionally and if he does, we'll certainly cater to him, in more ways than one. So, how to do it? That's why I'm here.

Seduction is a big word. Oh, boy, it reeks of soft porn and soft lighting. It also spells *l-u-s-t*. And no one these days can get enough of that. What can you do to seduce your girl? Why not set a date up at your house and romance her? And why should you do it? Because women love to be pampered as much as men love to have sex. Pamper her and get a wild and crazy night of hot sex. You game?

ELEMENTS NEEDED FOR SEDUCTION:

- Candlelight.
- A clean-shaven face. (As well as a clean body and a clean pad.)
- Some good food.
- A nice bottle of wine. Maybe even a good bottle of champagne to have after dinner.
- Nice music playing in the background. And by nice, I don't mean Kenny G.
- A willing partner.
- Some soft cushions on the floor.
- A bottle of scented oils with which to rub her.
- A classic movie like *Breakfast at Tiffany's*.

First off, cook a nice meal. It doesn't have to be anything with a special crème sauce; it can be a couple of choice steaks. (If she's vegetarian, cook something she can eat.) If you can't cook, order from a caterer and have a lavish table set for her with a nice set of silverware and dishes. If you don't have a nice set of any of this…you know what you have to do.

When she arrives, greet her at the door with a glass of wine, kiss her cheek and take her jacket. If she asks if she can help with anything say, "Oh, no, I've got it taken care of. You sit and relax."

I am telling you, saying something like this to a woman is the smartest thing a man can do. And it's also a good idea to tell her how good she looks. It's important to know that one reason women just don't jump in the sack with everyone is that they feel insecure about their bodies. Telling her how lovely she looks will help her build confidence about her body.

Once dinner is ready, sit down and serve her. That's right. Make a fuss over her, like you want everything to be just right. But if you drop a spoon or burn the steaks, laugh it off. This is supposed to be fun for *both* of you. (And if you do burn the steaks, order a pizza. You can still serve it on your nice plates and eat by candlelight.)

During dinner, as always, encourage her to talk about herself. How was her day? How was work? How was this and how was that? Smile often like you enjoy listening and add to the conversation about your day as well. Don't bring up the fact that your boss chewed you out over something, either. You can talk about that later. Keep it light and easy.

Now for dessert. Something really, really good and something really, really chocolate. You might want to buy it because making deserts is an art most of us don't practice. Give her the first slice and pick up her fork and ask if you can feed her the first bite. She should say yes. Feed her, hand her the fork and then eat yours.

We all know that the best part of the relationship is the beginning, when neither one of you can get enough of each other. Mmmm...*yum!* Just look at her like she is the only woman on earth. Wow. Makes any girl weak on the knees. Pay attention to her, to her needs. Ask if she would like more wine and pour her more wine. Little things add up. Paying attention to the details will make her know you are one special guy.

By now, both of you should be feeling it. Proceed into the living room where you have set the mood with candles. Why not buy a few nice, chenille throws and a few lush pillows for the floor? I think you should. Lead her over and sit down to watch a movie. Bring the bottle of wine and hit play.

And then let nature take its course. If she doesn't want a massage, pop the movie in, sit back and relax. And let her come to *you*.

WHAT WE LEARNED:
- Seduce a woman with wine, backrubs and good food.
- Make her feel special.
- In turn, she will make *you* feel special.

KEEP YOUR EYES TO YOURSELF

One of the main things that upset most women is when their man looks at other women. I know men look at other women all the time. I know it's your natural instinct. However, most women don't know this and think the reason you're looking at the other chick is because:

- She's prettier.
- Has bigger breasts.
- You like her better.

- You really don't want to be with her.
- You think that she's a big, fat ugly cow.

If this happens and she catches you, don't try to reason with her and don't tell her, "I wasn't looking at her!" She knows you were. Maybe explain it's just natural for men to do that (because it is) but don't expect her to buy it.

Or, maybe, just apologize and explain how much you care for her.

When you've been in a relationship for a while, stuff like this doesn't matter as much. For now, she is the only woman in the world. Treat her as such if you want to keep her.

Another thing: Just because you're going out regularly doesn't give you a full license to start treating her badly. Never pick doing something with your buddies over doing something with her, especially in first part of relationship. Women keep score like nobody's business.

WHAT WE LEARNED:
- Try not to be too obvious when looking at other women.
- If she catches you, shrug it off.
- Women can and will get very jealous over this sort of behavior.
- Don't start treating her badly just because you've been going out for a while.

WOMEN AND GIFTS

Women have a strange relationship with gifts. Most women want to know how you feel and how much you care. If you say it, it's good, but if you accentuate it with a small gift here and there, it's better.

Materialistic? Not at all. When we were living off the land way back in those cave man days, men would bring women things—meat, furs, firewood—and the women would have sex with these thoughtful men. Prostitution? Hardly. A way to live is more likely.

Today women don't need you to bring them meat or firewood. But they want to make sure you know how good you got it and one way to tell them is to buy them stuff. Don't like the sound of this? Live your life alone.

You don't have to spend much. Just a little something. A good box of chocolates, a bouquet of roses, good stuff like that.

This should be pointed out: Do *not* overindulge her. Just a little gift here and there, not something every single day or every week. Maybe once a month buy her something like a photography book or an artist's kit if she mentions wanting to paint. The point is to listen to what she's saying. She's dropping hints all the time about stuff she wants. And know that all women love those high-priced handbags. If you can afford a nice wallet or a purse or even a keychain at some point, you are going definitely going to get on her good side. (Only buy these things on the big days—Christmas, Valentine's or for her birthday. Also, keep the receipt in case she wants to trade it for another bag.)

Think your gifts through and if you can't come up with something good for her birthday—*which is the most important holiday of the year*—go buy her a gift certificate at the mall where she can spend it in any shop she likes. Make it for a good amount, too. Now for a very important message: When you present the gift certificate, buy her a funny or sweet card to go along with it. And when you present it, buy her a bouquet of flowers and a small box of chocolates. Put all of this into a nice gift bag and you will have a happy girl on your hands.

Or...

Tell her you would like to buy her some lingerie but don't know her size. Then go with her to the lingerie store and have her try on a few things. (It gets sexy in those dressing rooms, just let me tell you.) Let her pick out what she likes and then pay for it. After all, it's for you, too, isn't it? Well, it's mostly for you.

You can attempt to buy lingerie on your own but unless you're a smart man and steal one of her bras and a pair of panties to help you out once you hit the store, you'll probably end up getting the wrong size. (And don't ever steal a pair of her panties for other reasons, okay?)

Valentine's Day is a huge deal to women. You can buy her a gift but always, always include a card, some roses (a dozen is always good if you can afford it) and some form of chocolate. Also, a good meal is in order.

After you've been together a little while, know that it's time to spend a little extra. She wants jewelry and not something you got out of a bubble gum machine. Sure, at first this may be cute but if you give her something like this for her birthday, expect to catch it.

Diamonds. You can get a nice little ¼ carat pair of earrings for not that much in most jewelry shops at the malls around the holidays, especially Mother's Day. This is a nice little gift, but be warned, buying diamonds of any kind spells commitment. It might scare her off. Or it might make you think twice. If you don't want to buy diamonds, think gemstones—sapphires, rubies, etc.

Just think your gifts through and if you can't come up with anything, use a gift certificate. And you know to never, ever buy her a frying pan, right? If you do, expect her to chase you around the kitchen with it.

One last thing, make sure that the gifts are presented on the right days. If you give it to her early, you better make sure that you have something else for her on the actual holiday. And never give her anything late.

WHAT WE LEARNED:
- Women have a weird relationship with gifts.
- Buy her gifts but never overindulge her.
- Buy diamonds only after you've been seeing her for a while.
- If you can't think of anything, buy her a gift certificate for the mall.

JUGGLING TWO GIRLS AT ONCE

Good grief. This sounds like the plot for a romantic comedy gone awry. You are in some hot water now. For some reason, you've got two hotties interested in you at the exact same time. You can't decided which one you prefer, in fact, you like *both* of these chicks. I can hear you now: *Can I have both of them? Please? I promise to be real good!*

No, you can't. Who do you think you are? A rock star? Just because you feel like one doesn't mean you can act like one.

All I can tell you is that it will eventually blow up in you face. You can try the juggling act and it might work for a little while, but be a man and make a choice, otherwise, your women will make the choice for you and you might just find yourself alone.

WHAT WE LEARNED:
- If you try to juggle two girls at once, you've just asking for it.

IF YOU SCREW UP...

Being a man, women do expect this of you. Something will happen and you'll forget some anniversary or you'll say something she perceives as rude and then she'll be obligated to tear you a new one. Or, you might just get the silent treatment.

Whatever you do, if she's in love—or like—with you, she will forgive you—e*ventually*. But you will have to work for it, believe me. It will blow over after she's made you "pay" for a while. Women do this so you know she won't take any crap. It's a protective measure and a test. Women love giving men tests. I think just to see how badly they will fail. And then they grade you, rarely on a curve. Like I've said, ain't love a bitch?

I guess the point is that if you hurt your woman, you will live to rue the day and she might just turn into the evil bitch queen from hell. Women really get their feathers up when it comes to this stuff. But the key is to jump in when it happens and get it over with as soon as possible. Whatever you did, whether it was cheating or being rude, just apologize and ask forgiveness. Women are sensitive. Get used to this idea. But, hey, you can't live without them.

WHAT WE LEARNED:
- When you screw up, admit to it and ask for forgiveness.
- Eventually, she'll forget about it. Maybe.

EVERYBODY'S SOMEBODY'S FOOL

It's true. The time might come when you find out that your honey wants to break it off. In fact, she played you. She made a fool out of you. You once worshipped her and now you hate her guts. She dumped you after all you did for her. She gave you up even after you put up with her PMS!

I'm sorry, but it happens.

Don't go crazy. Have your feelings and then let them go and find yourself another woman. But always, always do this: Be the bigger person. Continue to be a gentleman. Don't let her know how she got to you. Revenge is a dish best served cold and when she sees you out with your new girl, she is going to be green with envy.

What if she cheated on you? Well, you know, it happens and it could happen to you. Cheating is a very sensitive subject, especially when you are in the beginning stages of a relationship because that's when you're pair bonding. So, to have her go out and do some other guy is really going to hurt.

My advice to you is to think long and hard. Don't go crazy with jealousy. It's going to be hard not to go a little bonkers, but try to keep yourself calm. She's human and she made a mistake, okay? If she leaves you for some other guy, then good riddance. She's probably going to cheat on him as well.

Maybe she just had a weak moment or got really drunk and the guy took advantage of her, so listen to what she has to say. I know you will be insane at this time and you're not going to be very reasonable. If you can find it in your heart to forgive her, forgive her. If you can get through this, your relationship will be stronger because of it.

If you can't get through it without calling her all kinds of hurtful names, then let her go. Don't ask her to stick around so you can emotionally abuse her. Why have all these big fights if you're going to end up breaking up anyway? Why risk hurting yourself—and her—more?

But know, we are all human and all of us make mistakes. If you really like this girl, you will find it in your heart to forgive her. And if you can be man enough to shrug it off as a mistake, then you're the kind of man every woman wants.

This is *not* to say that you should be a doormat. If she's a serial cheater and does it more than once, it might be best to cut her loose. As I have said, women do like sex as much as men and there are women out there who sleep around as much as men. I believe it's just in some people to cheat. Maybe your girl is one of the cheaters. Maybe she just can't help herself. But because she does this, don't do the old double standard thing and call her a whore or a slut. Men get away with this all the time and, just because she does it, doesn't necessarily mean she's a bad person. She just likes sex. A lot. Maybe you could try one of those open relationship things. And if that's not your bag, move on.

And a word about jealousy. You will find yourself getting jealous over her. That's okay but if you take it too far—by threatening her or accusing her of sleeping around—you really need to get some help. Love will inspire a little jealousy, but nothing over the top. It should come and if it does, feel it and let it go. Never let it get the best of you. If you start accusing her of things, she's going to walk out the door and never come back. You don't want that, do you? Only a truly insecure person will have a fit if he thinks his girl is checking out another guy. A real man smiles because knows she's going home with him. And if you always treat her right, you will have no reason to worry at all.

So, if something happens and you break up, take it as a life experience and move on. Be a man and let her go. If she comes back...you know the rest. Don't haggle her, don't cry and whine. Most importantly, don't stalk her! If she leaves you after all you've done, she is a bitch who doesn't know how good she had it. Once she realizes it, she might beg you to come back. And that will be your decision.

It's going to hurt for a while but think of all you've learned being with her. Apply all the good stuff to your next relationship and let some other woman reap the benefits.

WHAT WE LEARNED:
- Some relationships weren't meant to be.
- If it's not working out, move on and find another woman.
- If she cheats on you, ask yourself if you can forgive her and if not, don't put her through any kind of hell over it. Sometimes cheating is just about getting off and not about finding a new partner.
- Be careful with jealousy. If you find yourself in a mad rage, get away from your woman and cool off. Fights can sometimes escalate to the point of violence. *Never hit her.*

BREAKING UP

You found her, you dated her, you got laid. Now she's not jiving with you and your world and you want to dump her. Maybe you've got another girl you like better. Whatever the reason, who cares? You don't want to be in a relationship with this girl anymore and continuing on with it is pointless and destructive. And, if you don't like her but keep on dating her, that's, like, a bad thing to do. It's like you're lying to her.

Be a man and break it off before it goes any further. As with asking women out, there is no easy way to break up. For all you know, she wants to break up with you. But don't be a jerk and wait around for her to start hating your guts. Don't be a jerk and stop returning her calls or avoiding her. Make a clean break. Give her a call, tell her you don't want to see her anymore and expect a major butt chewing. Take it like a man and allow her to yell and scream for a good five minutes. Let her call you a slime ball and then be on your way. Tell her it was nice knowing her and you hope there is no hard feelings and then hang up and move on with your life. Believe me, this is the easiest way to go about it. Don't ever play mind games or any of that. Do it like a man.

Next!

WHAT WE LEARNED:
- If it's time to move on, let her know upfront. Don't play any stupid games like not retuning calls. Just tell her, "It's been nice but I need to move on. I'm breaking up with you."
- Be prepared for a big fight when you break up.
- Let her have her say and take it like a man, then excuse yourself and get on with your life.
- Always be a gentleman and she'll get over it.

THE THREE SCARIEST WORDS

I love you.

What fear that those three little words incite in men. It's like the scariest thing in the world. But you need to know that women want to hear this like nothing else. Knowing that you love her is better than a diamond ring. It really, really is. Nothing material can compare to the love-word. Nothing.

But how do you do it? Well, first you have to feel it and if you feel it, you will know it. Of course, saying it can be hard. Here's what one of my guys did. It was Valentine's Day. He got me a card with a rose on the cover that said, "P.S." Inside, was, "I love you."

That's how he did it. I was, like, shocked. But it was the sweetest thing he could do. Then he would slip it in here and there until I said it back. And that was about it.

Just be cautious and don't do it too soon. This will scare her off. Let it come naturally. When you feel it, say it and don't be afraid to say it. If she says it first, then you're off the hook. However, if she says it first, make sure to say it back *if* you feel it. And you don't feel it, man, you are in for the fight of your life and I can't help you with that. In fact, no one can. All I can do is tell you to duck for cover.

WHAT WE LEARNED:
- Saying "I love you" shouldn't be that big of a deal.
- When you feel it, say it. That way, if she doesn't feel it, you will know whether or not to continue the relationship.
- If you don't feel it, then let her know. That way, she'll know whether or not to continue the relationship.
- If you want to say it, say it, but never too soon.
- I think a good rule of thumb is by the second or third month of dating someone. If you're not feeling it by then, you might not ever.

YOUR WORST NIGHTMARE... *CAN WE TALK?*

I, as a woman, have a really hard time understanding why you boys don't like to talk. Sometimes when we say this, we're not looking to bust your balls. Granted, most of the time, we are, but occasionally we are looking for something else and that something could be anything from reassurance—"Of course you're the most beautiful girl in the world!"—to comfort—"Hold me, my tummy hurts."

Women want you to listen. Women love to talk more than men. It's biologically true; she uses a lot more words in a day than you do. She is a blabber-mouth. Let me tell you what to do: Take care of her and she will take care of you.

Keep in mind that the day may come when *you* want to talk and, if so, she might not be in the mood.

So, therefore, when your girl asks you to talk, you have not been cornered. Well, sometimes you have been, but let's just say she just wants to get something off her chest. Like are you going to make a commitment to her? I mean, she doesn't want to spend all this time with you if there's not a chance in you marrying her. It's true. It's time. It's that time and boy, you really need to make a decision fast.

So, my advice to you is to make your decision and tell her about it. If you don't want to marry her, be honest so she can dump you and find someone else before her eggs dry up. If you do want to commit but want to wait a while for marriage, tell her that. But if you make a promise, you better hold up on your end of the bargain. And don't drag it out, either. Be a man.

Another thing women do is ask loaded questions. This might be one reason men are scared when it comes to "talking." Say for instance, she asks one day, "Honey, do you think my butt looks fat?" You respond that no, it doesn't. In fact, it's perfect. Then the next thing you know, she's screaming at the top of her lungs at you. This is a loaded question. And she's asking it because, more than likely, she wants to start a fight. And there's a reason she wants to fight. It might be because you were rude to her mother on the phone. It might be because she caught you staring at another chick. It's probably because she's feeling insecure. Whatever it is, it will eventually come out. But not for a while.

Oh, boy. I feel for you when this happens.

Okay, fellas, women do ask loaded questions and there is no way to tell when one is loaded and when one isn't. And the only way you know it was a loaded question is if you get into a fight after a seemingly innocent remark.

When this happens, just sit there and let her go off. Don't block her out—listen to what she's saying because it's very important for her. Don't taunt her and don't start screaming back. Occasionally, take up for yourself and after she's calmed down, tell her, "I didn't say you have a fat butt. What's this really all about? Please tell me. I want to know."

One thing that you need to know is this: When she's going off for no reason, she might be PMSing. But if you ask her, "Is it that time of the month?" understand this will infuriate her even more. Sure, it might *be* that time of the month, but saying this is a one-way ticket to hell. She knows she's being irrational but she can't help herself. She doesn't want you to not take her seriously because of PMS.

So, let her yell and if she doesn't shut up within fifteen minutes, tell her, "I'm going to take a drive and let you cool off. When I get back, maybe you'll be a bit calmer and then we can talk about it." You're not walking away from her, you're just letting her cool off.

When you get back, if she's stilling wigging out, you might have a problem. Something really must be bothering her. Do your best to get it out of her and let her talk about it. If this doesn't work, I wouldn't recommend standing there and taking her crap for very long. Nobody deserves to be treated like this. Take a stand and tell her you're not going to put up with this. Women will try to push you around. They will try to push your buttons and they will try to hurt you by calling you lame names. If you don't stand up to her right then and there, you're facing a lifetime of being whipped.

Most times when women do this, they simply want to know that you'll stand up for yourself. If you don't respect yourself enough to do it, then why should she respect you? Stand up to her and let her know this isn't cool with you. Never disrespect her or, God forbid, hit her. Just let her know that she's just driving you crazy and you're not going to take it. Be firm about it, too.

WHAT WE LEARNED:
- When she wants to talk, let her talk.
- She will ask loaded questions and pick fights.
- Try not to engage her during these times and never ask if it's that time of the month.
- If she doesn't calm down within fifteen minutes or so, tell her you're going to give her a little breathing room and when you get back, you want to talk this whole thing out.
- Talk it out and then get the problem fixed.

- Sometimes, when women pick fights, they want to know that you'll stand up for yourself. Stand up for yourself and be firm. But never harm her when you're doing it. Always maintain respect.

WILL YOU MARRY ME?

So you've found The One. You want to make sure she doesn't get away so the obvious thing to do is ask her if she'd like to get hitched. How do you do it? Well, for starters, you say, "Will you marry me?"

If you want to do it in a special way, my suggestion is that you do it in private. That way, you don't put her on the spot in front of a huge crowd. And, you never know, she could say no. How embarrassing would that be?

Think back to your first date. What did you do? How about you repeat the date, from start to finish? Don't tell her that you're repeating the date and if she catches on with a, "Hey, this seems familiar," just smile and say, "Yeah, it's almost like déjà vu." But don't say a word.

As the date is coming to a close, take her back to your place, which you have stocked with flowers and candles. Once you're there, she'll know what's going on.

So, all you have to do is get down on one knee and ask her, "Would you like to get married? To me, I mean."

You don't have to do it this way, of course, but I think it's romantic. If you choose to do something clever, take a suggestion here and never, ever put an engagement ring in any kind of food. She could swallow or choke on it.

So what happens after you've popped the question and set a date? Don't worry. She will plan it all and all you have to do is show up. In fact, it's probably been planned for years.

Just a note: Before you ask anyone to marry you, it's a good idea to find out how much debt she's in. If she has a nice wardrobe, chances are, she's in debt. You need to find this stuff out because once you're hitched, you're in debt, too. Not that you shouldn't marry her if she's in over her head, but I think it's good to always be upfront and honest about all matters, including financial.

What if you're not getting married but want to move in together? Be prepared to change, boy. She doesn't want to pick up after you or cook every night. And all that clutter I told you to get rid of at the beginning of the book? It's time to do it.

Moving in together shouldn't be that big of a deal. In fact, it should save both of you money on your rent. The important thing to remember is to never take her for granted just because you've closed the deal by taking this step. Always take her out for dinner and continue to pay for it. Always buy her flowers and make a big deal out of her birthday. Treat her with respect and, occasionally, bring her breakfast in bed. Make your time together special. Most importantly, be a good man to her and, in turn, she will be a good woman to you. What else could you ever want?

WHAT WE LEARNED:

- When you ask her to marry you, do it in a special way that's memorable so she can look back and smile.
- It might be a good idea to see how badly your girl is in debt.
- If you want to move in with her, just ask her. This one shouldn't be a big deal at all and combining your resources can help the both of you save for a house or a nice vacation.
- After you've sealed the deal, continue to treat her like she's your girlfriend by taking her out for dinner and buying her gifts occasionally. Just because you put a ring on her finger does not make her your maid.

THE ENGAGEMENT RING

You did it. You asked her to marry her. Or you're planning on it. Or whatever. It's time to buy that ring that is going to set you back a pretty penny.

The ring might not seem like a big deal to you, but to women it is very important. They want one to show off and they want the best. If they don't get one, they feel like they've been cheated out of it.

Even if you can't afford a big one, you do need to get her something. Maybe tell her this is a promise ring until you can afford a better one. Let her know that you want her to know that you love her and want her to have the best, when you can better afford it.

This should be good enough and if it's not, she's a little too materialistic. Women know that not all men can afford a five carat diamond ring. Most women don't mind as long as they have the promise you'll do better when you can. If she's in love with you, that is.

But which one? White gold? Gold? Platinum? Listen to this. Unless you have immaculate taste, ask her friend or mother or sister to help you out.

You should expect to pay a lot of money for that itty-bitty thing but rest assured, if you don't buy her one, she will give you hell about it for the rest of your life. And if you can't afford one, why are you getting married?

WHAT WE LEARNED:
- If you do ask her to marry you and don't know what kind of ring to buy, go to her friend, mother or sister.

IS ALL THIS WORTH IT? I MEAN, REALLY?

Do you even have to ask? I mean, *come on.* Of course it's worth it! What are you? Some heartless jerk? I know what you're thinking, *What am I getting out of all this? It seems like a lot to go through just to get laid every once in a while.*

You just don't get it, do you?

Believe me, once you fall in love and/or become a dating machine, you will know the answer to that. However, there are some other perks involved as well.

So, what *do* you get out of all of this? She will become your number one ally, your number one fan. She will probably never worship you—at least not until there are no more cute boy bands in the world—but she will bring your life joy and passion and all that other good grown-up stuff you've been missing.

She will not, however, fix your life. She can't make you into a better man. That's *your* job. But she can help you to be a better man.

Once you've found your honey, your days will be like New Year's Eve. You'll want to celebrate for no reason. You'll want to kick up your heels and act the fool. You'll be telling everyone Merry Christmas, even in the summer. You'll feel like skipping like a little girl. Falling in love is just like make believe. It's the best damn feeling in the world and a feeling no one can get enough of.

Well, at least until the infatuation wears off. And that's another story. When you start having sex, you will never experience anything as nice as it is in the beginning. And most times, you won't even have to beg for it. There is nothing like falling in love and nothing like having the woman of your dreams love your back. It will blow your mind.

She's yours to have and to hold. She's yours. Get used to it.

But, you're saying, *but...it's still a lot of work.*

If she falls in love and marries you, she will be picking up after you for the rest of her life. Think about *that* before you start bitching about how much work this is. It isn't that much work to get the best thing in the world and call it your own.

Just know that when you get it, you'll always be warm in the winter. You'll have someone to ask you how your day was and give a damn if it went bad. You'll have someone to procreate with if you choose!

So, stop your bitching and get off that couch now and change your life. I don't care if you still think that there is no one out there for you. There *is* someone out there who wants you as much as you want them. Believe that and you're going to make the best boyfriend/husband around. Go on, now.

WHAT WE LEARNED:
- Nothing concerning dating or being with a woman is a waste of time.
- You can always learn a thing or two from each of the lassies you date.
- Falling in love with a woman, from what I've heard, makes you feel warm and fuzzy inside.

HOW TO BE THE MAN WOMEN WANT
The Get More Confidence and Meet Better Women
Guide To Dating

CONTENTS

WHAT THIS BOOK IS AND WHAT THIS BOOK ISN'T

This book is about becoming the best you can be. And it doesn't take much. What it does take is a willingness to look inside yourself and motivation to change. Change happens best when it comes from within. If you are ready to figure out why you aren't dating as much or as well as you'd like to, you've come to the right place.

This book is mainly about helping you overcome hindrances. We will look into issues of self-esteem, heartbreak and other things that might be holding you back. If you are willing to do the work required, you can and will overcome the obstacles that might be keeping you from being all you can be. This means you can become the man women want. And, after that, dating is easy. In fact, it will become like second-nature. If you can overcome some of your issues, you can rule your own dating life.

On the other hand, this book *isn't* about playing mind games with women. It's not about putting some spell on them to get them to sleep with you. It's not about playing tricks, using worthless pickup lines or mind control. This book isn't about making a fool out of yourself so a woman might pay attention to you.

It's about getting real.

This book is about looking at dating and, perhaps, yourself from a different viewpoint. It's about being willing to see dating in a different light. It's about being willing to see yourself in a different light. If, for some reason, you think you are a loser in love, you can definitely turn that around. And it all starts with you. If you can accept that you might be self-sabotaging yourself, you might be able to stop. This book will help show you how.

Keep in mind that what holds most people back from dating well is themselves. They get notions in their minds about what they can and cannot do. They have many self-imposed restrictions. This book tells you how to overcome these restrictions and get the dating life you want. Because, once you can overcome your restrictions, you can actually start doing what you most want—

dating well. One way to do that is to give yourself the respect you deserve. If you can start to respect yourself, then you can bet others will respect you, as well.

And isn't it time? Isn't it time to step up to the plate and take a swing? Isn't it time to start looking at dating from a different perspective? Wouldn't you like to view it as something to look forward to and to get excited about? That's the point of this book. It's about putting you in a different mindset. Some men almost break out into hives at the thought of approaching a woman. They don't have that needed confidence to follow through. And so, they retreat. This book is about teaching you how to have that confidence you need in order to approach and date women so retreat is the furthest thing from your mind. In fact, retreat will start to seem silly to you.

This book is about taking the fear out of dating. It's about learning that women aren't *that* unapproachable. Maybe it's just your approach that hasn't been working. If you knew how to do it better and how to get better results, wouldn't you do it? Sure, you would. And I hope to teach you how.

You need to know that this book, just like any book out there, isn't offering you instant gratification. It's mostly a wake-up call. *It's about getting real.* I am going to tell you how you can become the best you can be so you can get the best out of life. If you are willing and able to do so, come along for the ride. If this is something you really want, then all you need to know is that it is possible. It doesn't take much. But what it does take is a willingness to see things differently. And, mostly, it takes a willingness to see yourself differently. Once you can do that, you can become the man women want. You can be one of those guys that women love and desire.

And isn't that what you really and truly want? If so, read on.

ON BECOMING THE MAN WOMEN WANT

There are a lot of men out there who have no trouble whatsoever attracting women. They have what women want. They know how to talk to women, how to ask them on dates and they know how to actually *date* them so both parties get something out of the relationship. These men know women because they *like* women and they want to get to know them better.

Who are these men?

These are guys you probably know or know of. They are the guys in the clubs and at the parties that women flock to. They know how to make them smile, turn them on and get them interested. They are the men women want.

Why isn't this you?

Yeah, why not you? Why aren't you one of these guys? What is the difference between you and them? When you get right down to it, there's not much difference at all. The difference lies in the perspective. These guys are perceived differently from other guys. Therefore, they act differently and are received differently. They can do so much more than most guys and get away with a lot more, too. In fact, these guys are never lacking for a date and certainly never worry about getting a phone number. It doesn't even cross their minds to be uncomfortable about asking for a number. They aren't just playing the game of love; they are playing it well. They know it. The women they pursue know it. And everyone's happy.

Why?

Okay, look at one of these guys. Sure, he's pretty cute, but not movie star handsome. There's a certain boyish quality to him, or maybe even a manly quality to him that women dig. And all men have either one of these qualities. They're either boyishly charming or have a masculine attractiveness. Both of these qualities women adore. And you have one or the other, even if you don't recognize it.

Right now, figure out which one you have. And once you do, *own it.* You're either the boyish guy women adore or the masculine guy they love. Either quality is one worth having, so if you're boyish, don't worry about the masculine and vice versa. You are who you are, so own it right now. Embrace it.

Now, take another look at these guys. What are they doing that's so right? Why do women dig them so much when they don't even bat an eye at most other guys? What do they have that sets them apart? Are they super rich? Usually not. Do they drive big, fancy cars? Sometimes, but not always. Are they talented in some way the rest of you aren't? Nope. So what is it? Why them and not you? Well, why *not* them? I mean, why *can't* they do this? Why not?

Do you get it? Why *not* them? Why *can't* they be the men women want? Why not? Nobody ever told them *not* to be the man women want. But, most importantly, they never let anything stand in their way of attracting women. They don't let their lack of confidence or low self-esteem or any other issue they have get in their way of getting what they want.

So, now the question becomes: Why can't you be this guy?

Let's face it. You want to be that guy, don't you? I know you do. All guys do. All guys want to be that guy women love. The funny thing is, you can be that guy. Even better, it doesn't take much for you to be him. Well, keep in mind that it will take some work and some change in your attitude, but once you get these things taken care of, you will be the man women want.

And that's what this book is all about. It's about knowing that you can date whatever woman you want, within reason, of course. It's not going to be easy but that doesn't mean you have to make it hard. If you are willing to tweak yourself a little, if you are willing to be open to new ideas and if you are willing to listen to what I have to say, you can become the man women want.

But first, you have to commit. You also have to admit that it's time you make a change. If you already view yourself as perfect, then you don't need this book or any other advice anyone could give you. If you think you are prefect the way you are, then congratulations. You are one in a million.

But, on the other hand, if you are guy who really wants to get out of a dating slump, or even just to start dating in the first place, this book will help you get your dating life up off the ground.

This isn't about playing games. It's about getting out there and finding the woman—or women—you want to date. This isn't about putting out a false image of yourself hoping someone will latch on and love you for. It's about getting real and being honest and moving forward. It's about getting you ready—mentally and physically ready—to get out there and get the dating life you want. If you are stuck in a dating rut, hopefully you can overcome it by the end of this book. However, it is up to you to take the initiative to help yourself. All I can do is supply you with the tools.

Keep in mind that this book will be one hard truth after the other. And, as we all know, the truth hurts. However, the truth can and will set you free. The truth can help you overcome so many obstacles you might begin to wonder why you had issues to begin with. Nevertheless, if you're not ready to take on these challenges, then this book might not be the one for you. I am going to tell you how to be the man women want and I won't hold any punches in order to do so. In the end, I hope I will dispel some myths and, perhaps, some of your frustrations about the whole thing.

And that's all I'm going to say on that.

The most important thing I hope you will get from this book is that there is nothing wrong with you. You are not imperfect. You don't have to mold yourself into a different person in order to attract women. Sure, you do have to tweak and come to terms with some things, but it's not about changing your personality. It's about using what God gave you to land some hot babes.

You are not an unlovable person because you don't go out on many—or any—dates. What's wrong is probably the way you approach dating. If you can begin to approach it more realistically and a little less seriously, then you can become the man women want and, sometimes, women chase after.

Is that what you're after?

If you listen to my advice, there will soon be no stopping you. Once you get over looking at dating as a hassle and start looking at it as something fun to do in order to get to know others, you will begin to wonder why you thought it was a bother in the first place.

Like I said before, this book isn't going to offer you instant gratification. It is, however, offering you a wake-up call. I won't tell you how to play games or give you advice that doesn't work. I am just, simply, going to tell you know it's done. What you do with it then is up to you. You deserve the best, don't you? In order to get it, you just have to face some realities. And once that's done, you can get to the fun part—knowing what it's like to be the man women want.

ARE YOU READY?

In order to become the man women want, you must be ready. You must be ready to make changes and you must be ready to overcome your hindrances to these changes. This means getting over your heartbreak and resistance to change, which we will discuss later. This means setting aside any grievances and resentments you may have built up over time. This means getting over your hang-ups.

So, are you hung-up? Think about that. Having any sort of hang-up is like telling yourself you're going to be stuck forever. Having a hang-up on any issue in regards to dating is like putting a vibe out there that tells women you're a guy with issues. And that's one thing you don't want to be. Everyone has their own issues to contend with so most women don't want to get involved with a guy whose issues might eclipse her own.

It's not that difficult to overcome issues. All you have to do is first recognize that you *have* issues, or hang-ups, or whatever you want to call them. Once you do that, once you admit you have something going on that might be blocking you from happiness and a better dating life, you can see through the problem and to the solution. And once you do that, all you have to do in order to get over it is *release*. And all releasing entails is letting go.

Now the problem with releasing is that most people don't know how. One way to look at it is to think about something you really want but isn't happening. It could be to date a gorgeous woman, get a sports car or whatever. Take your pick. Now when this thing you want isn't within reach, it causes frustration, anger and a fair amount of anxiety. This isn't a good combination. If you are storing up this negative energy, any woman you come in contact with will pick up on it and probably not want anything to do with you.

However, if you take your desire and you release on it, it's got a much better chance of happening. But if you try to control the outcome of it, it's never going to be what you want. In a way, it's like you're saying, "I have to have this or that by this date and if it doesn't happen in precisely the way I want, I don't want it." This is a very constricted way of viewing things and full of control. This might just be the real reason you're not accomplishing your goals.

When you try to control the situation, what you most want suddenly becomes an impossible goal to attain. If you are feeling like this, you might not be ready to become the man woman want.

And you have to be ready. You have to be willing to release all your preconceived notions of what you think women want in a man and what you think you have to offer them. You have to get over any hang-ups you might have regarding whatever issue it is that you're mired down in.

All you have to do to overcome all this is to release. This doesn't mean to give up on what you want. It means to give up on the outcome of your desires. Sure, you might want a woman who is built like a fifties movie star, but what if a cute, flower-power chick enters your life and wants you? If you're hung up on the movie star, you won't see the flower chick and might miss out on a great love experience.

But if you release, then you will recognize when a great love enters your life and you will be willing to go for it. That's all it means to release. Release simply means getting out of your own way of happiness. It means to let go of control. Being ready to do this means *letting go* of control. It means giving yourself over to the process of finding good, true love. It means opening yourself up to the possibilities that might enter your life. And, most importantly, it means being open enough to recognize the possibilities that come along. It also means getting out of the way of your life and your success.

And all you have to do is release. Release the outcome and your preconceived notions. First of all, figure out what you want. Is it a long-term relationship? Is it a fling with an older woman? Is it just to go out and be comfortable in clubs and have a good time? Figure out exactly what you want and then... Forget about it. Let it percolate. And then the inspiration of how to do it will come to you. (You can use this with any aspect of your life, too, in regards to careers, housing or whatever.)

Of course, you might be afraid to release. A lot of people are. They think if they don't have total control over something, something bad might happen or something might go wrong or they might not get what they want. But they never realize none of us have total control. *We don't have total control!* Once you accept this truth, it might just open you up to the real possibilities of life.

When you find yourself in this sort of situation, you are letting fear guide you. Whenever you are afraid to let control go, that's just fear. This might be why you aren't dating as much—or as well—as you'd like to. If you try to control every single thing that happens, then you're not living in the moment and probably setting yourself up for a lifetime of disappointment. And you are *resisting* what you have and, thus, blocking what you want.

Resistance comes about because of fear. If you find yourself resisting anything in your life—from your job, car, apartment or the women you tend to meet—then you are basically saying, "I don't want this and until I get what I want, I won't have anything." And you find yourself in a miserable situation. Carl Jung said, "What we resist, persists." Think about that. If you are in a constant stare of resistance, have you noticed that everything tends to stay the same? Soon enough, you whole life is comprised of things you "don't want." When this happens, the resistance keeps building up. Once this happens, something has to change, right? And all you have to do is start releasing. That's it! Once you release, you will be ready to get out there and find the woman of your dreams. Until then, though, you're probably going to be a miserable person.

It doesn't have to be like that. If you want to be the man women want, let go of some of the control. Throw the reins aside and step down. You might be thinking, "That sounds great, but if I let go, she might just slip right out of my life." Again, the fear! So what if "she" takes a hike? Can't there be more than one "she?" Yes, there can be and there is! There are lots of women in the world, man! And most of them want a good man. Just because things didn't work out with her, doesn't mean another won't pop up in her place. This is called having faith. Just because the one thing you really, really want doesn't happen doesn't mean another good thing *won't* happen. And when you let go of control, you might just see that it does.

What do you have to lose? Nothing but waiting on some chick or whatever to materialize. Stop waiting and start enjoying! You have to be ready for this and being ready means letting go of control and just going with the flow.

So, figure out what you want. Release it. And live your life. Keep on truckin'! Don't hold out until something big comes along; take the small accomplishments and enjoy them.

And now, ask yourself: Am I ready? Am I ready to release all the hogwash that's been building up in my mind? Am I ready to move forward and find some good love? And, am I willing to do what's necessary in order to accomplish my goals?

If you answered yes, then you're ready. And that's the first step you need to take in order to get on with your life and live a happier existence.

HOPE

You've probably heard that saying, "Hope is the mother of all fools." I know I have. It's a saying that is loaded with desperation and disenchantment. Two things you don't want to find yourself in the throes of. But what if you've given up hope of ever meeting someone? Is that you? If so, it's time to get up off your butt and decide, once and for all, what you want out of life and out of a relationship.

I know it's hard, though. I know it's hard to keep trying only to get shot down. I know it's hard to even fantasize about meeting someone special. I know it can be difficult to go into a club or bar and look around and see yet another disheartening evening. And going in with that attitude, without much hope, can be a real downer. The trick is to ignite your hope once again and to go into these situations with renewed vigor.

So, ask yourself: What do I hope for? Can I do this? Do I even want to do this? Sure, it's hard to put yourself out there because of fear of getting shot down, but isn't it easier than being alone every single night of the week? Think about it. Which do you prefer? An evening which might be tinged with hope, with the possibility of meeting some hot babe? Or an evening of sitting home watching some dumb movie or playing video games?

It's your choice, you know?

How about this? How about instead of feeling dread about going out and meeting someone, you just don't have any expectations? How about just letting go of all that garbage stored inside of your brain from previous bad experiences and getting out there and just being seen? Sometimes just being seen is all it takes for some girl to zone in on you and pick you out of the crowd, especially if you're not trying too hard. She might just want to know what's up with you. Doesn't that give you hope? Good. Because that's what you need.

You need hope in order to proceed. If you have overcome your frustrations, you can see the silver lining in that dark cloud that may have just settled around your head. So, see through the dark and into the light. Feel yourself getting over the hopelessness of it all and see yourself going out there and having some fun.

Once you start to turn it around, you will start to see the possibilities that await you. And once you do that, you can become unstoppable.

THE GAME HAS CHANGED

Women aren't like they used to be, are they? Nope. They've changed. So what? Men have changed too. In fact, the world as we know it has changed. But it's not all bad, is it? What's bad is that while everything and everyone has changed, the rules of dating, the game in and of itself, hasn't changed much at all. Sure, it's been reworked and retooled, but mostly this is to no one's advantage.

The game of dating over the last few years has pretty much been skewered. Men and women alike are playing by a different set of rules than even their parents played by. Now we go to bars and clubs and speed dating and internet dating sites to find our new loves. Before, you'd just meet someone through a family member, in school or wherever. You'd meet, there would be an instant attraction and—bam!—you'd fall in love.

Or so the stories go.

Everything always seemed so much simpler back in the good old days. Of course, there were limited choices, too. It was a rarity that anyone would meet and marry someone from another country or whatever. So, while the dating game has changed, if you start to view it in a different light, you just might find it might have changed to your advantage. For starters, women can date and marry the men of their choosing without having to worry about what background he's from or what their parents might think or whatever. They're not so fixated on getting the perfect man, either. This means more freedom of choice. This means lots more hot babes to choose from.

See, it's not all bad news. Yes, the game has changed, but it still is focused on the same result—people getting together to have relationships. This is what the bottom line is.

So, in order to get over the newfound game of dating, one must first adhere to the new rules. And by this I mean, get over your hang-ups about dating through internet sites or speed dating or whatever. Open your eyes and your mind will follow. Soon, it will become like second nature.

The game of dating doesn't have to be difficult. It is what it is. And that's all it is. The problem is the frustration you might feel about it. And I know it can be frustrating. However, if you can overcome that frustration and get past your hang-ups, you can go on to enjoy a wealth of possibilities. It means that if you hand yourself over to the process instead of resisting it, you might just find that someone special you're looking for. And that's what it's all about.

Keep in mind that it doesn't have to be difficult. So don't make it difficult! Take the dating game for what it is, get up off your butt and get moving. Time is wasting, so don't waste yours. There are a lot of women out there just waiting for you.

HOT BABE MAGNET

There are a lot of men out there who are hot babe magnets. They are the very beings that women want. Women crave these guys. They fall all over them. They can't get enough of them. And that's what you want to become. You want to become a hot babe magnet.

So what *is* a hot babe magnet?

Think Steve McQueen. Think Rhett Butler. Think Don Draper. Think *Shaft*! These men are hot babe magnets. They know how to get women and they aren't afraid to get them. Of course, they're actors, playing fictional characters. But even so, study these guys. Find out what they're all about. One thing they all have in common is this: They like women. And they want women. And women return the favor.

Something else they've got? Confidence. They aren't intimidated by women in the least. They don't get fearful whenever they meet a new woman. *They only think of the possibilities.* So the secret of being a hot babe magnet is this: Don't be afraid to go after the woman you want.

Another good way to describe a hot babe magnet as being a man who always gets the woman he wants. He doesn't care how good looking she is, where she works, or what family she comes from or whatever. This is the woman he wants, and he'll have her. If not now, later.

Of course, this doesn't mean for you to be a stalker. There will probably be some women out there who you can't have. They might be married, uninterested, or whatever. This is just the way it is. The key is to not get hung up on one woman. If it doesn't work out, you move on and stop wasting time. A hot babe magnet knows this. He also knows that he's got something great to offer and if a particular woman can't see it, he will find another who can.

On the other side of this, look around at men that you think are hot babe magnets. Notice them in the bars and clubs or wherever. Study them. What do they have that you, perhaps, don't?

The hot babe magnet may or may not be the best looking guy around. He may or may not have the best body, either, or a fat bankroll. He's probably not drop-dead gorgeous. And yet, he's always going out with hot women. In fact, women love this guy. They can't get enough of him. So what does he have that you don't? Is he that special?

Maybe. Maybe not.

The main thing he's got is personality. Well, let me rephrase that. He's got a good personality. He's *comfortable* with himself. And while his personality might not gel with everyone else, he's comfortable with the one he's got and with who he is.

It sounds so simple, doesn't it? But it's true. This guy likes himself and, because of that, women like him. What's great about this is that you already have a personality, just like the rest of us. This means, you already have everything you need in order to become a hot babe magnet. You already have the power within yourself to do this. All you have to do is call it to the forefront and use it to your advantage. All you have to do is wake up and smell the coffee. And you start by admitting that *maybe* you could use a little help in this area. It starts by adjusting your attitude.

Sounds simple, doesn't it? And it is! However, I know some of you will read this and still find fault. You will lament, "But no matter what I do, they still don't seem to want me." Then what you've been doing must be wrong. If you can admit that, you can start to change and with change comes...*possibility*!

This book is about getting on with your life, getting through those self-pitying hurtles that always seem to hold you back. It's about getting out there, finding a good woman—or a few good women—and moving on with your life. If your life is at a standstill right now, it's more than likely due to your attitude. By adjusting your attitude and admitting that you might need a little help and then by accepting the help, you can move forward. And isn't that what you want to do?

Keep in mind, this will entail some effort on your part. Nothing comes that easy. If I could just wave a magic wand and change your life, I would. But I am not a fairy godmother. However, you are grown men and grown men accept responsibility for their lives. It's that simple.

You already have everything you need in order to attract women. What you need to do is bring out the best in yourself so you can have your pick of all the beautiful babes out there.

That's pretty much it, dude. Can you handle it? Or, as you read through this chapter, did you feel slight discomfort? If so, you've got some more work to do. The point of this book is to get you to the point where you *know* you can get a good woman. After you know, then you are ready to go out and find her. And once you're ready to go out and find her, you will have the confidence to follow through.

SETTLING FOR LESS?

Some guys have what I like to call the "low self-esteem" approach to dating. They don't care how a girl treats them as long as she agrees to go out with them. They don't care what they have to do in order to get her attention. They don't really care how much they have to lower themselves in order to keep a relationship.

In effect, they don't much care about themselves. They have the *low self-esteem approach* to dating.

I've seen it a lot, unfortunately. I've seen really good guys get a girlfriend who basically treats them like dirt. She acts like a total bitch and he sits there and allows it. He's just happy someone wants him. He has very low self-esteem.

The only problem with this is this: If you allow anyone to treat you like dirt, they always will. If you never stand up for yourself, people will run all over you. It's that simple. But why would you do this in the first place? Because you have low self-esteem.

Low self-esteem causes so much pain in this world it's unbelievable. At some point, most people are affected by it. However, there comes a time when you have to get over it and start feeling like the good person you are or you will face a lifetime imprisonment of taking other people's crap.

When you have low self-esteem, you not only settle for less, you *expect* to settle for less. It doesn't matter how hard you work to obtain what you have, you think you don't deserve it. Let me ask you this: If you don't deserve what you have, then who does? If you're the one who has worked hard for it, then why does someone else get all the credit?

The main problem when a guy has low self-esteem is this: Women don't like it. You're never going to be the guy women want if you don't think you're good enough to shine their shoes!

Also, having this problem can lead to settling for less of everything in life, including women. If you have low self-esteem, you will inevitably only attract women who will take advantage of you in some way. They're never going to love you for you when you have this problem. They're only going to love you for what you can do for them.

So, if this is you, how do you overcome it? How do you start to feel like a human being who deserves the best out of life? How do you get over your low self-esteem issues? Wow. That's hard, isn't it? And, yet, it isn't that hard. Yes, it's work, but if you're willing to put in the work, you can do. And all you have to do, first, is to recognize that you have this problem. I've always believed the saying that the part of the cure is in the actual diagnosis. And, second, all you have to do is take action to overcome it.

So, recognize that you have low self-esteem and then find ways to overcome it. It might take a few sessions with a therapist. Or it could be as simple as starting to see yourself for the good guy you really are. Instead of putting yourself down for all your shortcomings, look around and take pride in what you've accomplished in life. Know that, deep down, you are a good human being and that you do deserve to be treated like one.

On the other side of low self-esteem are the guys who think they have to put everyone down in the world in order to make themselves feel superior. They might brag about their higher education or sports car or whatever. And while they do this, they make cruel remarks to others who might not be as fortunate. If you are one of these guys, please do yourself a favor and take stock. People do not like people like this. And, keep in mind that most people won't look deeper into the real issue of your low self-esteem to see that what your problem is. They'll simply write you off and not like you very much.

In the end, low self-esteem will only end up biting you in the ass, in one way or another and you'll probably be too depressed or dejected to even know it. Just by taking stock of it and recognizing the problem, you can put yourself on the road to recovery. Keep in mind that it's okay to like yourself and, even better, it's fine to love yourself. Don't get hung up on what you don't have, but focus on what you do. Once you open yourself up to the possibilities, perhaps the door of opportunity will swing open for you. Have some faith.

WAITING FOR SOMETHING BETTER

This is also known as the "I am not settling for less!" syndrome.

Of course, it's not always bad to sit around and wait for someone better to come along, granted that they do, eventually, come along. However, some guys have been waiting for a long, long time. Are you still waiting for someone better?

This type of guy finds fault with every woman he's ever been involved with. She was too fat, or too loud, or she smoked or she had kids or whatever. He just can't commit to her because she's not exactly what he's been looking for. Trouble is, he can't really tell you—or even himself—what he wants out of woman because he doesn't even know.

This guy is in a vicious cycle of love 'em and leave 'em. But right about now, he may be beginning to realize that he needs to get moving before he gets too old. However, if he doesn't wake up and smell the coffee, he will be. That is, if he's lucky enough to get over himself in time.

So, he finds a woman, finds fault and then dumps her. And then he finds another, finds fault and then dumps her. And so on and so forth. What he fails to realize is that the fault does not lie in the women he's dating; it lies within himself.

Heavy, huh? It is.

The problem with having an attitude of, "I have to have the perfect woman or I won't settle," is that you might just end up alone. Women will eventually stop giving a guy like this a chance, especially after he reaches a certain age. When this happens, it's time to reconsider the problem of settling and start asking yourself if it might be you that's the problem and not the women you date.

Sure, everyone wants an ideal mate. They want them to be perfect in every single way. They develop the perfect fantasy of the perfect woman and the perfect life. Nothing is going to stop them from getting what they want. But something always does stop them and that something is reality.

People are not perfect. We all have faults. That's life. It's time to get over it.

Keep in mind that everyone has fantasies and there's nothing wrong with having fantasies. But when fantasies keep you from living real life, they're not fantasies any longer—they're a hindrance to life. If this is you, you really do need to pull yourself together before you become too fixated on the perfect woman. If you do that, keep in mind that soon enough, no ordinary woman will ever measure up to your exacting standards.

If you are still refusing to settle, ask yourself this: *What if my perfect woman never shows up?* And she might not. What if you never meet her? This is a hard reality to face, but by facing it, you are opening yourself up to the possibility of meeting someone pretty darn good. Sure, she might not be perfect, but guess what? You're not either.

You have to realize that this isn't about lowering your standards. It's about opening your eyes to reality and to the possibilities that exist in real life. If you have a fear of settling, then you're missing the point. The point is to find someone you can care about who will, in turn, care about you.

Know that if you try hard enough, you can always find fault in others. You can always find something wrong. We're all human and, as humans, we all have faults. Learning to accept this is the best thing you can do to gain a better relationship. By not looking for fault, you can be more of an accepting, compassionate and caring human being. The kind of guy any woman would be proud to call her boyfriend.

HEARTBREAKERS AND THE PAIN THEY CAUSE

Your past does not have to dictate your future, but for some of us, this is exactly what happens. You know what I mean, too. Something "bad" might have happened way back when that "scarred" you and now you can't move forward. You may be standing in your own way of moving forward because you're afraid it might happen again. Or, you may think, "Why bother attempting to do something because it didn't work out once before?" You're stuck. You don't know what to do.

It happens to the best of us.

However, in order to be the man women want, you have to get over all this stuff. It's a necessity. Past baggage is what might be standing in your way of getting what you want out of life.

There are several ways to describe this stuck feeling and they are feelings of just plain old disappointment or fear of future disappointment. But, mostly, it can be heartbreak. We've all been there. We've all done that. And, at one point or another, we've all let it trip us up. But we all have to move past it. We all have to get over our heartbreak.

It could have been a girl you lost to someone else. Or maybe she just broke up with you because she was a cold-hearted bitch. Who knows? But this one, this one chick, really did you in. You don't know how you can trust anyone else, right? But, the good news is, you can. And what if they hurt you too? Then that's life, man. Sucks sometimes, doesn't it? But if you never again open your heart to another woman because of one chick somewhere in your past, you will never again experience the true joy of living. And isn't that what you want? Don't you want to feel alive? Don't you want to tingle with excitement when you think about meeting a girl for dinner and a movie?

The other kind of heartbreak can occur from other people in our lives, people we once trusted. It could be a teacher, a former best friend or even a parent. Heartbreak comes in all forms and it doesn't necessarily have to be between a man and a woman.

It's happened to me and it's happened to just about everyone I know. It's called life and that's what happens in life sometimes. And when it happens, we have to reconcile the loss of our dreams, sometimes the loss of love from a friend. This can leave you with bitterness and resentment which, if not taken care of, can build up over time and rot your soul. I hate to put it that way, but I want my point to get made. And the point is that whenever we don't get over our past hurts, we only end up hurting ourselves, ultimately cheating ourselves out of life.

Of course, whenever we experience a loss of this caliber, we don't feel okay within ourselves. We think we have to compensate for the loss and find something that will make us feel better again. Once we can do that, all will be set back in order. Until then, we're not playing.

But it never quite works out like that, does it? All we get back is the feeling of lack that we are putting out. Soon enough, you might think to yourself, "How did my life turn out to be so awful?" And it turned out that way because you let one thing become a life altering event.

Sure, it can be hard not to turn hard and cold once someone betrays us. It's hard to put on a happy face and move forward. But what else can we do? How about if we consider the alternative? And what's that? Get over yourself and get moving with your life.

Yes, I know someone did you wrong and you might want to stay miserable to make them pay. Well, you're going to have to realize that your misery isn't having any effect on their lives, not usually. Usually, they come in, do their damage and go on, probably to damage someone else's life. And by you staying miserable, you're allowing this person to control you. You can't be in a good mood because so-and-so did so-and-so. What bologna! If they treated you badly and you let it hang you up, either they won't care, will feel good that you're still hung up over them or will think that you're pathetic for not moving on with your life.

Let me put it this way: When you're on your deathbed, do you want to look back over your life and realize that you've had a miserable time of it because so-and-so did such-and-such? If you can overcome this, things can be different. It's hanging on to this misery that keeps you down. But, it's letting go that frees you up to a better life.

You might not realize it, but heartbreak of this kind can taint any future relationship you might have, too. It can lead to repeating the same mistakes over and over. But it doesn't have to! You can get over it and you can move on. And how do you do it? You reconcile it, that's how. Sit down, feel your heartbreak and get over it. Allow whatever feeling you have to emerge, feel them and let them go. And then? You forgive.

Oh, boy, that's hard, isn't it? Forgiveness, which is one of life's great healers, is so hard for many of us to do. We just can't let go of that grudge, can we? We grit our teeth and shake our heads and... End up feeling like crap. That's all it leads to. But if you want to get over it, you have to forgive. You don't have to talk to this person again; you don't even have to tell them you're forgiving them. All you have to do is forgive. And how do you do that? By practice.

If you are ready to make this big step, all you have to do is this: "I forgive_____ for ____." And you fill in the blanks. It might feel a bit uncomfortable at first, so don't force it. Just say it in your mind. Think about what forgiveness means to you. Think about something you might have done to someone else and how you would like them to forgive you. Now take that feeling and apply it to the person you need to forgive. And once you forgive, you can let go. This is what you have to do to move on.

If you never forgive, you can't ever forget. And if you can't ever forget, you have to keep playing the same scenarios in your mind over and over, which, eventually, might drive you mad. But if you learn the art of forgiveness and really mean it when you do it, all that stuff that's been holding you back, making you bitter and giving you frustration will cease to exist.

Not a bad tradeoff, is it?

And, by doing this, you can learn a lot about yourself. You can look at your heartbreak as a learning experience and begin to really understand your boundaries and your sensibilities. You will learn what you will or won't put up with in the future.

By doing this, you will allow newer, better things into your life. But if you hold onto your heartbreak, you're basically asking for an unhappy life. And that's really not a fun way to live, now, is it?

FROM UNWANTED TO WANTED

It's happened to the best of us, believe me. You love her. She doesn't love you. She loves someone else. Or, maybe, she's just in love with herself. It is the universal problem of unrequited love.

Oh, geez.

When this happens, desire sets into your mind like cheddar cheese on a hot potato. You can't get her out of your mind. She's stuck there. You love her, for God's sake! *You love her.* Soon enough, she becomes an obsession and not in a sexy, perfume ad kind of way, either. She becomes an obsession in the sick-to-the stomach, incessant googling kind of way. But no matter what you do, you can't get her out of your brain. And, so, you begin to feel really badly about yourself.

What's a guy to do?

When you find yourself in love with someone who doesn't love you, it can be one of the most difficult things you can go through. It is emotional hell. There's no other way to describe it. You are, indeed, experiencing unrequited love.

If you find yourself in this position, it will not only make a fool out of you, but it might just keep a lot of good stuff form happening in your life. Essentially, unrequited love blocks real love from entering your life. It holds you back from living life to the fullest. It keeps you from meeting new women. And, mostly, it just makes you plain miserable.

But what can you do? You're in the throes of an unrequited love affair! How do you get yourself out of this mess? Well, the best thing you can do whenever you find yourself in this position is to give up on the girl who's caused it. You have to release her. And then, once you've done that, you can move on. Yes, it will be hard. Yes, there is some pain involved, but once you're over her, you can move on to someone better.

Yes, you can.

One reason people get caught up in unrequited love is because they believe this person is perfect for them. They believe this is the one person in the world who will give them everything they've ever wanted—all the good sex and good feelings that comes from the good love. But, unfortunately, this isn't going to happen. Ever. It's done. It's over. Put a fork in it.

One of the best things you can do right now is to recognize what you're doing to yourself. You are putting undue stress on yourself by hanging on when you should have let go. However, if you can let it go and move on, you can go from being unwanted to being wanted.

When you're in this position, you are blocking new women from coming your way. Basically because you're off the market, mentally speaking. And if you're off the market, you can't date anyone else. By getting over her as quickly and as smoothly as possible, you are opening yourself up to newer, better experiences. And once you do that, you can move on. Once you do that, you might just look back and wonder how you got so hung up in the first place. Then you can go from being unwanted to wanted. And usually all it takes is recognizing what you're doing and then stop doing it. Refuse to google her. Refuse to think about her. Wash her out of your hair, man! Get her out of your system. Make a vow to get over her—today—and move on what your life. Let her go her own way and you go yours. And start right now.

Breaking an obsession of any kind is hard, but if you're diligent with it, it can be done. And mostly it just takes refocusing your attention on something constructive. So, refocus and get her out of your hair. And then get ready to move on. There are other women out there just waiting on you to get over her.

So, are you about ready to meet them or not?

IT'S TIME TO GET OVER YOURSELF

One way to get on the road to becoming the man women want is to clean your slate. And by this I mean, clear out anything in your past that might be holding you back from becoming the man you are supposed to be.

Imagine a big chalk board and write on that board everything that bothers you. Write down previous mistakes and girlfriends who treated you badly. Write down all your regrets and issues. Write as much or as little as you need to. And then what? Wipe them clean. That's right, clean off all the resentment you might have because of these things. Clean off all the mistakes. Clean off every single thing that is holding you back. Get as close to a perfectly content state as possible.

The things that happened way-back-when don't have to haunt you day in and day out. What's the big deal if your last girl dumped you? It means you weren't compatible and she did you a big favor. *Yes, she did.* Even though it might still hurt and you might still feel that sting of rejection, by her doing this, she has saved you a lot of trouble. She's someone else's problem now. This means there is someone out there who is better for you.

Now, imagine wiping everything off—all those bad dates and blunders and embarrassing moments. All those bad relationships, or hit or miss ones. Wipe off all the chicks that blew you off. Forget about the ones who might have used you. Take away any cringe moments you might have just because at that time, you probably weren't using good judgment for whatever reason.

All these things are in your past and that's where they should remain—a distant memory. You don't have to keep reliving them and making yourself feel bad. You don't have to settle for less or stop trying to date just because of something that happened. It's time to stop punishing yourself. And, seriously, that's pretty much what you're doing when you relive all this stuff. So, stop doing it.

The next step is to erase all you've been taught about women and dating by the media, your friends and, even, your parents. Yes, all these people may have had good intentions, but it might not have been the best advice for you. Just take away whatever advice that wasn't necessarily in your best interest and keep what you need. Clear your mind of the mumbo-jumbo and set yourself free.

Another thing to get rid of is all the romantic movies you might have seen. All the fairy tale stuff that really doesn't mesh with reality. Wipe away any preconceptions about what dating "should" be like and begin to accept it for what it really is—a way to meet someone special. Wipe away the notion of settling for less, or, even, waiting for something better.

Once that's done, wipe away anything others might have told you that put you down. If someone said you were fat or ugly or just plain not good enough, wipe it off. You are starting with a clean slate and you don't need this anymore. Getting rid of this will boost your self-esteem and that's what we're after. So, forget about anyone who made you feel badly about yourself. *Don't let them stop you from moving forward.*

Now that you're done, the best thing you can do is to make your own rules to dating. Yup, that's right. Think about what you want to do and then do it. Make your own rules to getting the woman you want. You and you alone know what's best for you. Make your rules by using the guidelines in this book, but shape them into whatever works best for you. Keep in mind that everyone is different and this means that what works well for some, might not work for others.

Most importantly, know that from now on, you are in control of your own destiny. This means, you have to take the blame away from everyone else and take complete and total responsibility for yourself. Today is the day that you start anew. And you can do that once you clean your slate. This will rid you of all your encumbrances and allow you to start fresh.

And, lastly, if you have any issues dealing with money—bankruptcy, etc.—it's always a good idea to work on that before you bring someone new into your life. Get your finances straight so you can focus on what's really important and that is finding the woman of your dreams.

So, say bye-bye to the old you by cleaning your slate and hello to the new you—becoming the man women want.

STOP WORRYING ABOUT GETTING LAID

I know one of the main incentives of dating for men is sex. Surprise, surprise. *Shocker!* I understand this is a big deal for you guys. Having said that let me say this: Stop worrying about it so much!

The problem with always having sex on the brain is that when you do, you go into any situation involving the opposite sex with an agenda. Your agenda, obviously, is to get laid. And the problem with this is that it puts you in a one-down position with women. It also reeks of desperation and, even if you think you're not giving off that vibe, women can smell it a mile away.

Desperation isn't a good look for anyone. It's a big turn-off. However, for some, they don't even know when they're being desperate. But if you go into every situation thinking about sex and obsessing over it, then you will come off as being desperate. Your hormones are always in overdrive. You're probably a little jittery and nervous and this will come off as just plain creepy to the women you meet.

The main problem with this is that when you think like this, you risk coming off as being needy and no chick really wants a needy guy. When you come off as *having* to get laid, it makes women cringe. They wonder, "What is up with this guy?" And, "Uh, no, he wants something from me. Best to nip this in the bud right now." And then they get turned off from you.

Essentially, it puts them in a position where they are *expected* to fork over something they may not be ready to fork over. Think of it this way: Have you ever been walking down the street and you see someone who is trying to sell something? If you're not looking to buy anything right then, you will avoid this person. Right? You know whatever they're selling you don't really need or even want. So, you sidestep them and walk on. It's the same principal. If a woman knows that all you want from her is sex, she is going to sidestep you, just as you would the vendor on the street.

Now I know there are a lot of books out there that tell you how to get women into bed. They offer a lot of empty promises and can make you look like a creep, or, at the very least, a fool. Sure, you can use these techniques and maybe even get lucky—possibly one time out of a thousand. But what you're not going to get is any sort of fulfilling relationship. And I know that might not be what you're after. Maybe all you want is to just get laid. If this is your end-all-be-all, then why not ask yourself why. Is it that important? Are you going to die if you don't have sex soon?

Well, let me tell you, if you actually put in the time to get to know a woman in the way I am telling you, you stand a helluva better chance of getting laid than you would using some sort of pick-up method. You could try that for years before it works. This way works more quickly, but you do have to be willing to commit to someone. You have to be willing to respect women as human beings. And if all you want is a quick roll in the hay, you're not giving them any sort of respect. Women know this. That's why they avoid guys who only want sex.

One reason you might be thinking about getting laid so much is because of all the over-sexed teen comedies out nowadays. In these movies, total losers find women who are so pretty and so horny they can't help but get laid. This may have put some false expectations in your mind—*if he can do it, so can I.* Well, hate to tell you, but "he" is a fictitious character and what works for a movie subplot won't ever work in reality. These movies are fun to watch, sure. But just be entertained by them. Don't make them into a life plan.

You have to know that women aren't really looking to get laid all that much. Yes, they do like sex as much as men, but mostly in the confines of a relationship. This is because of the possibility of pregnancy. If she gets knocked up with some guy she just met, well, what's she going to do? She doesn't know this guy. She doesn't know if he even wants—or likes—kids. This puts her in a pretty pickle. If she gets pregnant, she's got a big headache. What's the guy who got her pregnant got? He might end up with a guilty conscience, but he isn't committed to doing anything. He can walk off, Scott-free. After all, he's not the one who's pregnant, now, is he?

Can you see my point? If you look at it this way, you might understand why women aren't just jumping into bed with every man they run across. You might understand why pick-up tactics don't usually work. And you might even begin to relax a little and take the pressure of getting laid off of yourself. So what if you don't get laid soon? The world is not going to end.

And this brings us back to my point. If all women think you want is sex, they won't want to get to know you better. They know if they give it up that night, you will probably be gone in the morning. This puts a wall up between you and them. And it will be hard to mount that wall once it goes up.

Sure, sure, I know you probably know some guy who gets laid left and right with no strings attached. He's probably out whooping it up all the time. Big deal. After a while, however, all he will be able to do is have sex. He won't know how to have a real relationship. However, once he hits a certain age, he won't even be able to have sex that much, either. Once he gets older, he won't be as fun as he once was. And one of the main reasons this guy gets laid is that he's probably around a lot of very drunk women. Or, he's around women just like him.

Remember, sex is a very personal experience and many women don't want to give it up just because of that. They only want to give it up to a guy they know isn't being desperate and to a guy who isn't expecting it as some sort of payment for dinner or whatever.

Women like strong men and being strong entails getting your hormones under control. I wish there were a more delicate way to put this, but there isn't. So, when you make overtures at someone in hopes of getting laid, you are at risk as being seen as suspect and partly disingenuous. And that leads to looking needy. No one wants that. Do you? Of course not.

All you have to do to get this situation under control is monitor yourself a bit. This doesn't mean to change your whole personality or demeanor. It just means to put a lid on the whole "I need sex and I need sex now and that is making me feel very needy and desperate" situation. Remember, when you're out, you're just out to have a good time, just like anyone else. If it leads to something, then it does. If it doesn't, you won't be crushed or angry about it. This puts you into a whole different category with women. You're the cool guy; you don't care if she gives it up to you or not. This lends itself to mystery and women love mystery. It is a huge aphrodisiac to women.

Once you get this under control, you will have women wondering what is up with you. They will think, "He's very interesting, but somewhat aloof. Yet, he doesn't seem interested in me in that way. What's up with that? Hmmm…"

Do you see how this works? It works by letting them know that while you are interested, you're not so interested that another girl can't come along and turn your head. This sparks interest in them and they will want you all to their selves.

In essence: If you act like your life depends on some chick making it with you, you'll never find one who will. However, if you pull back and act like you can take it or leave it, there might be more than a few takers. All this entails is that you get your mind off getting laid and not putting out that desperate vibe. This means, just go out to go out and have fun. Go out to meet some new people. And don't go out with the sole intention of getting laid.

REMEMBER WHEN…?

Once you begin to get over all your hurdles and start to become the man women want, you will have a good reason to get out there and find those women who are waiting for you. You might even begin to look forward to it, too. Can you remember a time when dating was fun and exciting? It used to be fun and exciting, didn't it? It used to be something that you just did instead of something you felt obligated to do. You weren't stressed about it, were you? You weren't "on the hunt" then so much, were you? It wasn't a dire, life or death situation. It was just a time that you just went out, had some fun and didn't have any expectations. In essence, you were in the flow.

Before you got older, didn't you and your buddies go out and have fun? Didn't girls sometimes join in on the fun? Can't you remember when you kept it light and airy and didn't give a hoot if you hooked up or out—you were just out having a good time, after all. Think about that time when there was no pressure to find "The One." Remember when it was just fun to go out and shoot some pool or have a beer or whatever with the guys. Remember when you didn't have any expectations. Remember when you were just out being yourself and how much more fun you had.

Think about it. I am sure it wasn't that long ago. And think about this again: *Remember when you were just out being yourself*

27

and how much more fun you had. This is the feeling you need to reclaim. That feeling is what is going to make you more attractive to women. You need to be just a guy out and about having a good time and not really looking for anything. You're open. That's the important thing. You are open to new experiences but at the same time, you're not looking for them.

The most important thing I can stress is this: *Just being yourself will attract women like nothing else.* Think about that for a moment. I want it to sink in. Got it? Good. Let's repeat for emphasis: *Just being yourself will attract women like nothing else.* Women will want to get to know you because you look free—problem free, trouble free, carefree, and free to new opportunities. They'll see you out there having fun and want to know what's going on with you. Why? Because they want to have fun, too. They will want to join your party.

If you can learn to accept yourself, others will automatically accept you. No one is out there trying to change you. Well, maybe your mom is, but that's a different subject for a different book. But, seriously, no one wants you to be something you're not. If it's you that's trying to be someone that you're not, then just stop doing it. Stop trying to change yourself and accept yourself for who you are. You were given a distinct personality. That's what you were born with and to try to alter it is a recipe for disaster. You won't go far pretending to be someone you're not. In fact, you won't get anywhere.

It's important to never give someone a false image of what you think they want. Always give them the real you. So what if you're a little shy around new women? Women love shy men! They see them as a challenge. So what if you get a little loud after a few drinks? Lots of people do. And so what if you come across someone who doesn't like you for you? If she doesn't like you for who you are, she never will. Don't morph into what you think she wants just to get her attention. Just be yourself and wait until someone comes along who will like you for the unique human being you are. And don't doubt that it will someday happen, either. I've seen it happen to guys with such low self-esteem, it's a wonder they could even get out of bed in the morning.

Once you can be yourself, then you can become the man women want. Just be yourself, just be the man you are meant to be. If you've heard something about how women only like a certain kind of man, then you've heard wrong. Women like all kinds of men, but they especially like those who like and accept themselves for who they are. Don't adjust yourself in order to meet someone's criteria. Just allow things to happen naturally. Do not ever try to be this or that because you think it might work better. It never does.

Just be yourself. That's all anyone expects anyway.

DON'T BE AFRAID TO LOOK HER IN THE EYE

It's all in the way you act, really. It's about treating a woman like she is a woman. Women like to be treated nicely by men, but they don't want a man to act like a wimp or a pushover. They want someone who is willing to go out on a limb and address them. They want a man who acts like a man. So, be the man and approach that woman. And treat her nice. Give her the respect she deserves. And, most importantly, look her in the eye.

Making eye contact is crucial. This lets her know you're not shifty or hiding something. It also lets her know you're comfortable enough with yourself to do that. It lets her know you are, indeed, a man.

If you have trouble with this, it is more than likely due to a self confidence issue, which we will discuss later. I think one good way to figure out if you do have issues with confidence is the degree to which you look people in the eye. If you look around and find that you can't make eye contact, you might have low self-esteem.

And that's not so good; especially if you want to date. Women like men who are confident. Just as men like women who are confident. They want a man who can look them in the eye and be certain of himself.

Let me put it this way: If you can't look her in the eye in the first place, what chance do you have when she wants to pull you into conversation? Not much. Showing her that you're unafraid of how she's going to react to you—by looking her in the eye—lets her know you're a guy who knows what he wants and is willing to take the chance.

So, ask yourself this: Am I willing to take the chance?

KEEP IT LIGHT

If there's one thing most women hate is a guy with no sense of humor. Sure, she might be an art chick who goes for the brooding guy with the dark side at first, but he's going to wear thin after a while. Most women, generally speaking, like to laugh and they love men who can make them laugh.

Dating can be so serious but it doesn't have to be. If you learn to keep it light and airy, then you can attract more women. One way you do this is by taking yourself less seriously. Also, by taking the seriousness out of dating, i.e. the desperation, you can open yourself up to a whole new group of women who just want to have some fun.

Just by relaxing and acting cool as a cucumber, you can keep it light. By not taking everything so seriously, you can attract women who will want to know you better mostly because you're so easy to be with. If you can be comfortable with yourself you will automatically make her more comfortable with you. And that's what you're after.

THE AGGRESSIVE MAN

Women know that men are the pursuers. Women like this fact and use it to their advantage. However, what they don't like is an overly aggressive man, a man who chases and never stops, even when he has been told to. They don't like it when a man becomes obsessed.

You're not this man, are you?

In order to be the man women want, one thing that you can't do is be overly aggressive. Sure, if you see a woman you like and want to give a little chase then go for it. But a little chase simply means being the one who initiates a conversation. It doesn't mean to literally chase her down the street or stalk her.

How can you tell if you're too aggressive? You zero in on a chick and stalk her like prey. Or, if you get her attention, you won't let go of it. You might use forceful body language and stare intensely in her eyes. When you do this, it makes women very uncomfortable and makes them want to bolt.

Sure, sure, we know that most everywhere in the animal kingdom the male has to chase the female. It doesn't take a genius to figure that out. However, while a little chase is great, too much equals a sad, lonely night of television and a TV dinner.

Keep in mind that you will have to put some work into getting a woman. But if you find the perfect one and then hunt her down, you're just going to scare her off. Of course, I understand you don't want her to get away. She *might* have forgotten to call you. Maybe. However, you can't let your impatience get in the way. If you do this, you end up not only looking like a fool and but also kind of creepy.

If this is you, all you have to do in order to correct this is to monitor your behavior. You should have an outgoing personality without being too aggressive. So what can you do? You do what feels right. Keep in mind that every woman is different and what works with one will not work with another. Always listen to your gut. If you have a feeling you might be making her uncomfortable, then back off. This will save you a lot of trouble and embarrassment. Also, watch her body language. Is she leaning forward or is she leaning back? If she's leaning forward towards you, she's interested. If she's leaning back, not so much. That's an indicator to step away for a while.

Another good way to understand this is to simply put yourself in her shoes. If you are unsure if you're acting inappropriately, then think about how you would feel if someone were doing this to you. By putting yourself in her situation, you will begin to understand the dynamics of your actions. And then you can correct them so you don't come across badly.

Being too aggressive is never good. It can make you look desperate and we've already talked about that. So, just take a chill pill, listen to your gut and then *chill out.* If she gets away, there's more where she came from. But being aggressive will not only scare her away, it will never make you the man women want.

SHOW JUST ENOUGH INTEREST

Are you interested in getting someone to really like you? If so, one of the main things you can do is to show just *enough* interest. Then you leave them wanting more.

It's not hard to do. Say you meet some hot woman at a party or whatever. You're really, really into her, aren't you? Well, don't show it! Stand around and engage her in conversation for a while, then excuse yourself. Now, don't go back to her for a little bit. Let her watch you, let her get antsy about if and when you're going to come back over. Let her sit for a few minutes. And while you're doing this, if she is interested in you at all, she will wonder what is up with you. This will spark desire because desire comes from wanting something we can't have. If you put yourself into a position of being desirable, all the work is done for you. All you have to do is show up.

Now this does not mean to treat her like dirt or ignore her or whatever. It just means to hold back a little and let her come to you. This leaves her wanting more. It makes her wonder what you're all about. If you can leave a girl wanting more, you can have her.

Many men, for some reason, just don't get this. They think they have to be all over a girl—sometimes any girl will do—and if they keep on her, they'll wear her down and she'll have sex with them. (We discussed the desperation about getting laid earlier.) This is a totally inaccurate way to think. No, you will not wear her down and get into her pants. All you will do is annoy her and ruin her good time.

Now, on the flip side of this, if you meet her, talk with her for a few moments, then disengage yourself, she will think you don't really like her. This will make her wonder why. And it will, in turn, make her want you. Of course, this isn't the case for every single woman out there and every situation you may become involved with. But it will work for most. Use this at your discretion and with women you really like. You don't want to use it on just anyone because if you do, chances are they're going to really like you and if you really don't like them, there will be a big mess to clean up. I'd suggest avoiding this at all costs.

Here are a few tips:
- Never gush or go on about how good she looks.
- Don't ask personal questions.
- Never laugh at a dumb joke—just chuckle.
- And, never, ever show too much interest. Show just enough.

A few words on the last tip, "never, ever show too much interest." If you show someone you're really interested, they will bolt. I've seen it happen time and time again. The odd thing with women is that if you let them in on the fact that you really dig them, they get scared. It's almost like they think you're ready to commit to China patterns and baby strollers. (Yes, some women are as commitment phobic as some of you guys.) This sends up warning signs in her mind and she starts thinking about nightmare scenarios.

Don't ask me why. This is just the way it is. There isn't much logic in the game of love.

On the other hand, if you can learn to hold back, give her some space and not show how much you like her at first, then you've got it in the bag. She's probably going to dig the space and respect you are giving her. This lends itself to trust and with women, trust is a big issue.

You might be wondering how, exactly, you do this. How do you leave them wanting more? Because you have confidence in yourself and you don't come off as desperate and you don't fawn over them, most women you come in contact with are going to want more if you act in this manner. Remember, the chick you've just met is cool—and pretty damn hot—but so what? There are a lot of cool and hot chicks in this world. She's just one, right? This is the attitude you need, even if you do feel butterflies in your stomach. Even if you are so attracted to her you can't stand it. You just need to hold back and reel her in slowly. Never let her know how much you're into her. Soon enough, you will have her hooked and you can reel her in. But take your time in doing so!

This doesn't mean that once you get her phone number you play silly games about calling her. This is about you getting her interest sparked in you. Once that happens, play it like a cool guy, not a douche bag. You don't want to piss her off too early in the game, but neither do you want to crowd her. If you say you're going to call her, then call her. If you ask her out for a date, then show up on time and then take her out and show her a good time.

Keep in mind that this isn't a hard thing to do. Keep a little distance but never be an asshole. Soon enough, she'll be eating out of your hand. Once you've got her hooked, then you can let her in on how you feel. But always leave her wanting more.

HOW TO GET THEM INTERESTED IN YOU

And now for one of the most important lessons in this book. How do you get chicks interested in you? It's easy and kinda funny—you get them interested in you *by acting like you're not interested in them*. To be more specific, you act like you're slightly interested but not *too* much. Yeah, you think she's cute and all that, but you've got things to do. She might be fun to hang around, but so what? Other girls are, too.

If you can master this skill, you can inspire women to want to get to know you. If you can do this, they do most of the work for you. All you have to do is show up, act like a nice guy and keep it cool. This makes them wonder if there is something special about you. Why aren't you falling all over yourself for them? What's so special about you? They won't know and by you holding back, it will make them want to know.

This goes without saying, but I am not saying to act like some jerk who thinks all he has to do is hang back and the women will flock to him. No, you will have to approach women, but you just can't be too eager with them. Yes, you might have to buy a few drinks; you just don't buy them *all* their drinks. You give them a little rope, but never too much that makes them think you're a pushover. Women like a challenge and if you can be seen as a challenge, you can have your pick.

If you're unsure of what I am saying, let me say it again. The more interested you act, the more they will back away. They might feel like you're smothering them. However, the less interested you act, the more they will want you. It's like they're saying, "Hey, I know I'm pretty hot, so why isn't he into me? Have I done something? Have I not shown enough interest? What is going on here?"

It sounds crazy, doesn't it? Well, it might be crazy, but it's the truth.

Women think that if you're too interested in them you might be a loser. They might look at you as some guy who can't get any chicks, so they don't want to get stuck with you. That's why a lot of women won't talk to you when you approach them. However, by acting not all that interested, you can pretty much bet that they're going to want to know what's up with you. And, soon

34

enough, when you get all the preliminary stuff out of the way, they will know.

THE ROCK STAR PRINCIPLE

Women don't really want men to be easy. This is what we discussed in the previous chapter. If you're too gushing or too nice, they end up thinking something is wrong with you. It's like you're on clearance or something. Harsh reality, but true. And if you come on too strong, you end up looking desperate. But what is a guy to do? What can a guy do to let women know he's alive? He can act like a rock star.

Pick your favorite rock star. And if you don't like rock music, just pick your favorite country, opera or whatever star. Think about this guy. What is it about him that's so great? He's rich, of course, and probably somewhat talented. And, most importantly, he's a friggin' rock star! *Hello!*

But, seriously, this guy, this dude, Mr. Rocker, what is so darn special about him anyway? He never has to work for women. He just has them land in his lap. And plenty of them, too. And women, even when they know they might not have a chance with this guy, will do anything to get him. They all want a rock star. *Always.* And they want him because he's pretty much unattainable. Therefore, he's worth fighting for, worth making a fool out of themselves for and worth being turned down by.

He's a rock star. And guess what? You can be one, too.

No, I am not telling you to get the band back together or learn to play the guitar. Unless, of course that's what you want to do. I am telling you that you can take this guy's attitude and use it for yourself. I can hear you say, "But I'm not cool enough! This guy is cool!" But you can be cool, too! This is about building confidence, which is the most important thing you can do. If you can become more confident, you will become a man women want. Confidence builds over time, but it is important to start laying the groundwork now.

Everyone has good qualities. Right? And if you look at rock stars, you will see that they do too, but they might not be the best looking guys on earth. But they are confident. They are self-assured and a man who is confident and self-assured will go a long way with women. You are cool enough to be a rock star even if you can't drink copious amounts of whiskey. If you think you're not cool enough, you will never be cool enough. Having confidence is nothing more than telling yourself you're just as good as all these other dudes. And you are! You can be a rock star with women!

Never—ever!—underestimate yourself or your worth. That's what gets so many people into trouble and sows the seeds of self-doubt. You know that you have good qualities, so play on them. If you can afford some new threads, go buy some. If you can't be a rock star, at least dress like one. Well, maybe not. Some of them dress like they found their clothes in a garbage can.

The point is, every single person in this world has had their confidence tested at some point. And some more than others. It's time to get over it! Claim your confidence and your right to be a cool rock star guy and then go for it. With confidence, nothing can stop you. If you think that you are the best, most everyone else will think you're the best too.

Of course, I am not talking about being arrogant. No, no, no. Arrogance and confidence are two totally different things. With confidence, you've got the goods to back up the swagger. With arrogance, you don't and you're hiding behind a façade. And soon enough, the gig will be up.

So, the best way to become the man women want is to get a little confidence. I know it can be a challenge, but it is so worth investing in. Do whatever you have to in order to build confidence and then watch the ladies flock to you. Just as if you were, indeed, a rock star. And, if you don't particularly want to emulate a rock star, just emulate other confident men, whether they are successful business men or cowboys or whatever. It doesn't matter who, just as long as you do.

THE IMPORTANCE OF FIRST IMPRESSIONS

"You never get a second chance to make a first impression." How many times have you heard that one? Think about what it means. It means that what you first present to someone upon meeting them is the lasting image they will have in their mind of you, pretty much forever. If you present a cool confidence, that's the way they will think of you. However, if you present an aura of nervousness, then that's they way you will be viewed.

Oddly enough, the importance of first impressions is overlooked time and time again. Even when they're going out of town, some guys still go out of the house looking like they just rolled out of bed. And then they lament about how hard it is to get a date. The thing is, if you don't care how you look, how can you expect anyone else to care? You can't.

But it's not only appearances that are important to making a good first impression. If you meet someone and start off by putting yourself down, even if you are just using self-deprecating humor, they will always look at you in the way you portrayed yourself. For example, if someone compliments you on your hair and you reply, "My hair? It's awful, full of cowlicks. I can't ever do anything with it." Then that person will always view you as the guy with cowlicks. The image you put out of yourself, especially to women, is the image they will always have of you. It is rare that you will come across a person who overlooks this and sees that you're just putting yourself down and then feels sorry for you or whatever. They will really think of you as the guy with cowlicks. This is why it is so important to portray an image of self confidence.

People who are confident within themselves would never put themselves down for any reason in front of another person. And other people rarely think badly of them. In fact, this person with the high self-esteem might evoke some jealously from others because they can see how much they truly like themselves.

You should keep in mind that whenever you first meet people, they aren't looking for fault in you. Most often it is our "bad" self images that we project and this projection is how people will see us. In essence: What we give them is what they get. And if we give them a bad first impression, that's what they'll always have of us.

If you know this might be a problem area for you, then all you have to do in order to stop is to become aware of it. Once you are aware of how you present yourself to others, you can correct this behavior by simply catching yourself when you do it. For instance, if someone gives you a compliment, accept the compliment and respond back with a "Thank you." If you're the kind of person who responds back with a, "Well, yeah, but…" then you are, more than likely, giving off bad first impressions. This also makes you seem not very confident. The reason for this is simple: If you can't take a compliment from someone you know, then it's pretty obvious you won't be able to take one from a complete stranger. What's more obvious is that because you view yourself in a "lesser" way than others, you won't be able to make a good first impression.

When you are trying to become the man women want, a good first impression is key. Without it, there will rarely be a relationship to speak of. It just won't go beyond that awkward introduction. If you find yourself putting yourself down for any reason, stop. I mean it—stop! Stop it right now! Maybe you use this sort of self-deprecating humor as an icebreaker or whatever. No good. Just don't use it at all. If you have to put yourself down in the hopes that others will like you, then those people who would respond well to it aren't the kind any self respecting person would want to find themselves in the company of.

So, once you realize how big first impressions are, you can start to make them. Use this to your advantage. By displaying an image of self confidence, you are not only letting these women know that you like yourself and enjoy your own company, but that they will, too.

LOOKING FOR LOVE?

Have you ever lost something and could not, for the life of you, find it? Let's say it was your keys and God knows that this happens to all of us. Where did they go? You search your place from one corner to another, to come up with nothing. And guess what? They are exactly where you left them. *But this is usually only after you've almost given up looking for them.*

Looking for love is kinda like looking for lost keys. The more you try to find love, the harder it is. Have you ever noticed that? The harder you try to meet someone, the more elusive the idea of actually doing it becomes.

You might be thinking, "But if I don't actually look for love, how am I ever gonna find it?" And I would reply, *the answer is in the question.*

Looking for love, just like looking for lost keys, means that you are trying too hard. If you try too hard to find something, it rarely happens. But once you are just about to give up, it happens, almost like magic.

Most people I know tell me that they met their loves when they weren't looking. They were too busy, had too many plans and blah, blah, blah. And then—bam! They found the one they'd always been looking for. It sounds like a romantic comedy or something doesn't it? Well, that's because that's usually how it happens.

It's just that when you look too hard for love, the less likely you will find it. And why is that? It's because you are concentrating on the *looking* and not on the *finding*. This doesn't mean to give up on love. Oh, no, that's not what I'm saying at all. What I am saying is to relax a little bit on it. Chill out some. And let it evolve naturally.

All humans want love. That's all we want. We want to be loved and we want to give our love to others. It's just that sometimes it doesn't evolve quite so naturally as boy meets girl, falls in love, gets married and so on and so forth. Sometimes it's boy meets girl and then gets his heart broken and then get transferred across the country for his job and so on and so forth. Just because love doesn't follow a linear path doesn't mean you should give up on it.

I understand that there is some panic involved in finding love. It's like we want love and we want it now and we think we have to force something into happening. We feel like if we don't try our hardest to do something, it won't ever come about. But if you think about it, it never happens anyway. So why panic? Why hunt love down like a wild animal? Why not sit back and let it happen on its own?

Take internet dating. Everyone's doing it, right? However, if you go into it with any sort of desperation—*I must find the woman I want online!*—then you are looking too hard for that perfect match. The idea is that while you're looking, you're not getting hung-up on the ideal. You're just seeing who's out there. You're releasing the outcome.

Remember we talked about releasing? That's all you're doing here. Just release what you want and see it come to you. Stop looking and watch it happen. In an odd way, it's almost like you have to give up on it before it comes knocking on your door. This is, in essence, letting go of control. And once you can learn to do that, you can make anything happen, mostly by just wanting it to happen, but not getting hung up on the where, when and how.

Sometimes, you can be your own worst enemy. You can stand in your own way of happiness without even knowing it. If you are desperate for love and need it, you will, more than likely, turn off any potential dates. This is because you're putting out a vibe of desperation. You might not even be aware you're doing it, either. But once you get desperate, you can block anything from coming into your life. It's like you're putting up a wall between yourself and what you want.

The great thing is that all you have to do in order to turn all this around is to stop being desperate, stop looking for love and start having a positive attitude. Remember, most everything is in your attitude. How you feel about things comes across to those you meet. Sure, having a good, positive attitude may sound kind of hokey, but it's the one thing you can do in order to get the most out of life. If you know what you want and know that you deserve it, getting into a positive mindset is usually all it takes in order to attain it.

Pretty cool concept, huh?

WHAT, EXACTLY, DO YOU WANT?

In order to become the man women want, you have to know exactly what you want in the first place. If it's a soul mate, then so be it. If it's to date around with a few different women at any given time, so be it.

If you don't know what you want, then how can you ever hope to get it? It seems easy enough, though, doesn't it? Knowing what you want? But many people don't have a clue as to what they want or why they want it. They just know they're lacking something, though they can't put a finger on what it is.

Right now, think about what you want. Seriously. Stop reading for a moment and think about what you want. Be precise. Be specific. And then write it down. Write down every single thing you want. Now look at the list. That shouldn't be too hard to do, should it?

Knowing what you want is paramount in actually *getting* what you want. If you are uncertain about what you want, then how can you ever expect to have your wish granted?

On the other side of this is the important issue of knowing what you *don't* want. Knowing what you don't want is just as important—if not more so—then knowing what you do. So think about this, too. What don't you want? Obviously, a girlfriend who cheats. Maybe not to be stuck in dating hell? Any and all of those things that brings up feeling of negativity is a don't. Write them down, too.

Now that you've figured out what you don't want and what you do, you can actually start to make this stuff happen. Whenever you think about what you want, feel it. See yourself meeting that perfect girl. See yourself on that great date. See yourself being confident and self-assured. See all the things that you want to happen, happen. This is the fun part! Isn't it great to be at this part? So, have fun with it.

This isn't a terribly difficult process, so don't make it one. It should be viewed as like going into your favorite store and buying all the things you want. It's like you're a kid in a candy store again. Be that kid and have fun, even if it's only in your mind right now. Soon enough, it will be in your reality.

So, have fun with it. Make the transition from what you don't want to what you do want. And sit back and watch your life transform.

THE LAZY BOY COMFORT ZONE

It's hard, I know, to get up out of your recliner and do something. It's hard to envision a future of hot chicks. It's hard, I know it's so hard, to turn off the TV, dust the potato chip crumbs off yourself and go into the world and see what you can do. Sometimes it's just so easy to sit back and let life pass you by.

Is this you? Have you found yourself in the lazy boy comfort zone?

Sure, I know you want more out of life. Hell, most of us do. I know you want something better. But, hey, knowing doesn't make it so, brother. You might be looking out the window with some trepidation and a little unease. Life can be better, but what if it never is?

Oh, boy, now I'm depressed, too.

Come on! Get up and get going! Your life is waiting on you! Are you kidding me with this? I think what this is called is feeling sorry for yourself. And, hate to break it to you, but no one wants to be around someone like that.

The day does come when you have to make a choice. You can either sit back and let life pass you by, or you can get up and get to it. The day comes when you have to spread your wings and fly. Sure, everyone wants better, but it's having the cojones to do better for yourself that might be making you a little apprehensive. This feeling of unease comes about because you might just be in a comfort zone. It's a complacent place. It's nice and warm. There's nothing wrong with being comfortable. The problem lies in the fact that comfort zones can take years out of your life. And when you look back and see that all you've done is worked, napped and watched TV, you might get pretty pissed off at yourself.

Is this you? If so, admit it. You don't have to do anything about it, of course, but admitting it is the first step towards curing it. I understand that looking towards the future and envisioning a better life can be a little scary. Hey, it's scary for everyone, not just you. Sometimes it *is* easier just to sit back and let things ride. It can be scary to start looking for a new love. But it doesn't mean you shouldn't do it. It just means you're human. That's all.

Ironically, comfort zones are rarely comfortable. Fear tends to take over when we find ourselves in them. When we're not out trying new things and meeting new people, we begin to think we can't ever do these things. And it gets easier to sit back and let life pass by.

You have to realize that the only way to a better life is to take that first step into the unknown. And this can cause some anxiety. If this is what you're feeling, then you've probably been in the comfort zone way too long. You like what you have now. But don't you want to love what you have? Wouldn't that be so much nicer? But you have to be ready to get that love. Until you're ready, it probably won't happen.

The other problem with comfort zones is that this is where many people get stuck. You get stuck in an okay job and with okay friends and with an okay apartment. Everything is *okay*. It's just *okay*. You might not want to get out of your routine because you just don't want to have to think too much about anything. You've probably worked really hard to get where you are now. You don't want to give it up. But the thing is, you don't have to give anything up in order to get better. All you have to do is get out of your comfort zone and be ready for new experiences.

Ask yourself this: While it's all well and good to stay in the comfort zone, is this really what you want?

Think about this: Wouldn't it be great to find that dream girl? Wouldn't it be nice to go out and be the life of the party? Or, maybe, even just be invited to a party? Hell, yeah, it would be! It would be so nice! Thinking about stuff like this should excite you enough to get up and do something about your situation. If it doesn't, then you are definitely stuck in the comfort zone and not too far from giving up. But don't do it! Don't give up! Giving up on life is for losers and you are not a loser. If you were, you wouldn't have picked up this book. I know that and you know it. If you were a loser, you would have already conceded to a monotonous life. And I'd be willing to bet that you are far from doing that.

It's time for you to get excited about your new life. It's time to overcome any anxiety you might be feeling. It's time to drop your trepidations and get out there and get going. And you can start right now. All you have to do is feel the excitement of what's in store for you. Think of all that wonderful stuff that is going to happen soon. And once you do that, not only will your future look brighter, but your *now* will, too.

ARE YOU LIVING IN REALITY?

Many people, women included, have preconceived notions of what love, romance and relationships should be about. They have an idea that it's supposed to be *this way* and if it's not *this way*, they can't handle it. If it's not perfect, then there's something wrong.

What you might not understand is that life isn't a romantic comedy, or even a comedy of any sort. Life is just life and it's meant to be lived. What this means is that if you have an idea of the way things are *supposed* to be, you might not be living in reality.

With women, there's the ideal of Mr. Right. All women want this guy. And he's the perfect guy who does everything right and never makes a mistake. If he does make a mistake, then he atones for it and everything goes back to being picture perfect.

Men do this too. They have an ideal Miss Right, as well. She's just the other side of Mr. Right but, obviously, is a woman. She's got a great body, a great personality, can hang with your friends and watch football for hours on end and she doesn't care if you call her or not. She can slam a beer and cook a turkey with no effort whatsoever. Miss Right is every man's dream. And that's all she is—a dream, a fantasy men have conjured up to escape reality.

There's nothing wrong with wanting someone perfect for you. It's when you want someone prefect that you tend to get in trouble. Women, like men, aren't prefect. Sometimes they don't want to hang out with your friends and sometimes they might get upset because you forgot to call.

So, right now, ask yourself this: Am I waiting for Miss Right? Seriously, are you? And you do know that she doesn't exist, right? I hate to tell you, dude, but it's time to wake up and smell the espresso. If you are serious about meeting someone special, or dating some special girls, you have to get over your ideal Miss Right.

The problem might be that we've all been a little fooled by Hollywood. We forget that Hollywood manufactures dreams, not reality. Not only do they have romantic comedies for women displaying the perfect man, they give men the idea that there are perfect women in this world if only they could find them. And that's the rub right there—finding this perfect woman. It's like looking for a needle in a haystack when there was no needle in there to begin with.

Everyone buys into this ideal because it sounds so good. You get a cool chick, who is not only stacked, but allows you be you without any sort of responsibility. When this perfect woman never shows up, you end up feeling horrible about your life and wondering why no woman ever measures up to your ideal.

Movies aren't based in reality. But you think that if you wait long enough for this perfect woman, you will find her and live happily ever after. But you won't. She doesn't exist. But maybe the real reason you're waiting is because you see what's on the screen and feel like your life doesn't compare. It isn't as good as the characters in the movies and on TV. In fact, it's downright mundane. You might even think that your life is boring, so you need a girl like that to come in and liven things up a bit.

Many people have been so brainwashed by the media, any "normal" person will have trouble cutting it with them. Men want the perfect woman and women want the prefect man. So, each gender begins to turn their noses up at the opportunities in their lives and wait for something better. And they're going to be waiting a long, long time.

We've been told by the media to always stay young and never settle for less. Unfortunately, if no one ever settles, no one is ever going to get married, have kids and keep the universe going. If we never settle, we can never experience the true joy of being with someone who, simply, asks us how our day was.

So, it might be a good idea to come to terms with all this. There is no Miss Right, but there is a *Miss Right For You*. There is a woman who will love you for you. It's time to face facts and those facts are that women are human and they don't have superpowers and they can't live up to anyone's unrealistic expectations.

If you have these unrealistic expectations, it might be time to do a reality check. This could be a big reason you don't date as much as you'd like. This is about you making a conscious effort to get out there and get a good woman. It's about becoming the man women want and that means facing the reality of the situation: Women are just women, just as men are just men.

And isn't it time? Isn't it time to stop waiting and to start taking action? So, get over it and find yourself a real woman. It's definitely time to do that. Right?

BEING WORTH IT

You might be beginning to think that a lot of the advice in this book centers on self-esteem. And you'd be right. Having good self-esteem—i.e. confidence—is what we're after. I believe that having these qualities helps a person get anything in life that they're after—from finding a great girl to getting the best pay.

One indicator that you are on the right track in life is knowing that you are worth it. This means that you know that the good things in life are within reach and, once you're able to obtain them, you can. The problem lies in the belief that you aren't worth it, that you don't deserve the best in life. If you think you're not worth it, if you think you don't deserve any of these great things life has to offer, you won't be. You have to feel like you are worth something in order for others to think you are, too. If you think you're not worth anything, you're fighting a losing battle.

If you have confidence, you don't think about things like whether or not you deserve something. You already know you do. And you know you do because you've put the time in for it. This doesn't mean that you think you're entitled to it just because you're so great; that's not what I'm talking about. But then again, maybe it is.

Have you ever noticed those people who seem like they're entitled? They always get the best out of life and that's because they don't expect any less. They do have a sense of entitlement but, then again, they always get what they want. These people always seem to be happy, too, and they're happy because they know that the things they want in life are obtainable and that they do deserve the best.

Do you think like this? If not, you might not be able to become the man women want. You might not be able to bring up that confidence you need in order to go through with dating the women you want to date. But all you have to do to turn this around is to recognize this hidden belief that you may have that you're not worthy and that you don't deserve the best. If you can recognize it, then you can do something about it. Then you get it out of your system, step over it and start living the life you want.

So, what you have to do is get it in your mind that you are worth it. You are worth a pretty girl taking the time to get to know you. You are worth having a better job, car, house or whatever. If you can start to believe this and get over your low self-esteem, you can begin to obtain all that might have seen elusive.

I think most problems in life start with your attitude. If you carry around the attitude that you're not worth anything and that you're a low human being, so you shall be. You have to overcome this in order to be more open to the opportunities that will come your way. And, if you can do this, you can get over the desperation. You can overcome the feeling of lack and of doing without. You can let things go.

Once you can do this, women will want to get to know you better. It's inevitable. Being the man women want means being worth it. If they see you as having worth, they're going to want to latch onto you. However, if you don't see yourself as having worth, they never will, either.

Get it into your mind that you are one cool dude. You're hot, man! You're a rock star! You are worth some chick taking the time to talk to you and go out with you. You are worth having them flirt with you and getting to know you better. Don't be afraid to ask for what you want and if it's a hot chick, then so be it. You want a hot chick! And you deserve one, too.

Being worth it also means being choosy. You don't have to stick with a girl that might make you feel bad about yourself. You have a right to be picky. But this doesn't mean to be *too* picky. This doesn't mean to tear a woman down once you get her and bail at the first sign of imperfection. Just understanding that you are a hot commodity and tapping into what you have to offer—being a good guy who cares or whatever—is all you need to be worth it. And all this entails is that you start believing you are worth the effort.

And you are, you know?

DESPERATE IS AS DESPERATE DOES

I know we've covered being desperate several times in this book already, but I want to touch on a few more things before we move on. So, let's get it out of the way: Don't be desperate.

This might not even apply to you. I hope it doesn't. But if it does, you might want to consider the reality of what it's like to be desperate. I have seen a lot of men who will put up with a lot of headaches from women just because they're afraid of being alone or whatever. It's pretty obvious why these guys do this—they're insecure and don't think they deserve any better. And this makes them desperate and allows women to walk all over them and treat them in a not so nice way.

There is no need for you to ever be desperate. It will cause nothing but problems.

If you want to be the man women want, you have to get over being desperate. Ironically enough, once you stop being desperate, women will usually start giving you the respect you deserve. I know where the desperation comes from and it comes from a sense of feeling inadequate combined with the panic of being alone. It's a pretty simple combination that amounts to a lot of misery. Of course you don't want to end up alone but that doesn't mean to get desperate and allow women to walk all over you. It means that you're aware that you need to do something about your situation and that you'd like to eventually get married and, perhaps, have a family. Hey, that's great! These are the things most normal people want. And if you put in the effort to obtain these goals, you will probably end up getting what you want. But if you're desperate about it, you're probably going to end up with someone who walks all over you.

Understand that the woman you choose will be a big influence on how the rest of your life turns out. If this woman doesn't respect you to begin with, she's probably going to nag you all the time about everything in the world once you're together. Do you want that? I didn't think so.

Of course, this doesn't mean to pass on every woman you meet because you might fear she will walk all over you. No. It just means letting her know to begin with what you will and won't put up with. This also means that if you do start dating a great girl, don't push yourself on her. Be cool about it, hold back and allow the relationship to evolve at its own pace. If you bug someone too much in the beginning, they will eventually find a way out of the relationship. If you call more than a few times a week during the early stages of the relationship, you will come off as being desperate. Then she will start treating you bad in hopes you will break it off with her so she won't have to go to the trouble herself. Harsh truth, but that's just the reality of the situation.

So, just think about how desperation might be playing a role in your dating style. If it is, it's time to nip it in the bud and start believing that you don't have to be desperate in order to date a hot babe.

TIPS ON SUCCESSFUL DATING

It's pretty simple to become the man women want. It's also not that hard to have success in dating. But, in order to do this, you have to define what you want, what you are willing to put up with and the lengths you're willing to go. Or, on the other hand, what you're *not* willing to put up with and the lengths you *won't* go.

Can't think of anything off the top of your head? Never fear. I have a list.

To become the man women want, it's a good idea to...

- Have boundaries. What will you put up with and what won't you put up with? What if she's perpetually late? What if she hates your friends? What if she makes fun of your dog?
- Communicate your boundaries. Once you establish your boundaries, don't be afraid to let her know about them. This lets her know you won't be anybody's doormat. Now, if you want to be someone's booty call, that's entirely up to you.
- Establish what you want out of a woman, out of a relationship and out of life. Write it out. If it's a home and family, good for you. If it's to play the field, then okay. However, defining this is a must in order to achieve it.
- You have to have confidence. When a guy is confident in himself, he's the man! A guy with confidence never reeks of desperation and doesn't fear leaving the party alone. He just goes with the flow. A confident man doesn't need a woman in his life, but never rules out the possibility of dating one.
- Watch your drinking. Drinking too much can make fools out of even the best men. So, be careful not to use alcohol not as a social stimulant.
- Keep in mind that every woman you meet might not be looking to settle down. So, if marriage and commitment scare you, you're in good company because it scares a lot of women, too. However, if this is what you're looking for, don't get too upset when you find someone who doesn't want the same thing. Just keep trying until you do.
- Relationships are work. Any one you might get involved with will be work. You have to be willing to work at relationships.

- Never, ever be afraid to get out of a bad relationship. Even if she's the prettiest thing you've ever laid eyes on. If you end up marrying this chick, she will probably make you miserable. If you can't live without her, just be prepared.

These are just some suggestions. You might already have a list yourself and it might be somewhat different than this one. That's okay. You can add or take away the things that apply to you and your personal dating style. The point is to open your mind so you can expand your horizons. This is a simple guideline, but understand these are the things that can help make you successful at dating. And that's what we're after, buddy.

THE PRETTY ONES ARE ALWAYS THE CRAZIEST

For some reason, crazy always comes hand in hand with pretty. Have you ever noticed this? The most attractive women always seem to have a screw loose somewhere. But that's what makes them so interesting. Right?

But you men just love them, don't you? Crazy girls are just the bomb! They can stir it up and keep it fun. The crazy girl is the female equivalent to the bad boy. Women love bad boys and you men love your crazy girls.

I tend to agree. Crazy girls *are* interesting. Sure, she's fun. She's exciting! But what if she gets a crazy idea about burning down someone's house or knocking over a liquor store? She could, you know. They don't call her crazy for no reason.

If you are the sort of guy who is very attracted to the crazy girl, it might be time to ask yourself why. I can understand that you might want to "save" her, but my question here would be: Why not save yourself? If you get too overly involved with a crazy girl, she is going to suck a lot of life and time away from you. And she can't help it. That's just the way she is. As fun and as exciting as she can be—in the beginning—it will start to wear thin after a while. Because crazy is as crazy does. And crazy does a lot of crazy stuff.

Finding yourself in a relationship with a crazy girl will do one of two things: Give you the excitement you need or the heart attack you don't.

The only problem with dating a crazy girl is that you will waste a lot of time in a relationship like this and it will emotionally— sometimes financially—bankrupt you. And it will keep you off the market for better women. Better women won't go near you if they think you're involved with a crazy girl. They will stay away because once a crazy girl becomes a crazy ex-girlfriend, she will drive both of you out of your minds. Therefore, she will haunt any new relationship you might have.

Of course, I am not saying all good looking women are crazy. No, no. I am saying that you guys sometimes just see the pretty and not the crazy. Of course, you know she's a little off when you start seeing her, but damn it! She's so pretty! You can't take your eyes off her. Understandable. But what happens when the fun and excitement wears off? You're stuck with her. And all the crazy things she does.

So, is she worth it?

Usually, not. But give the girl some credit. She's just doing what come naturally. However, if you can avoid her, my advice would be to do that very thing. And if you've already got her in your life, just be careful. If you're lucky, she'll get bored with you and go on to torture someone else.

WOMEN ARE NOT BITCHES

One thing that will stand in your way of becoming the man women want is a bad attitude. And if you go into any situation involving women where you have the attitude that all women are bitches, you're going to fail.

Sure, sure, I know some women are bitches. It comes with the territory. I also know that some women *can* be bitches. No surprise there. But, mostly, women want what men want and that's love. They want to be loved for who they are—bad moods and all. This doesn't mean they hate men and it doesn't mean they would rather stay single for the rest of eternity than to succumb to a man, it just means that, sometimes, they get tired and frustrated. Some of them just get tired of playing men's games and some of them get tired of being the casualty some guy's commitment phobia. This, among other things, can make them a bit hard-nosed and difficult to deal with.

As we all know, dating can be hard. It can be hard to get out there and try, try again. But if we never attempt to do it, then we have nothing to look forward to in life but the new fall television schedule. A bit sad, isn't it?

The point is if you want to be the man that women want, you have to like women. Sure, you don't have to put up with bitches that make you feel terrible about yourself or whatever. But being with a woman will entail some overlooking of her mood swings from time to time.

Of course, there are those women out there who think the worse you treat a guy, the better he will be to you. I think they call this "be mean to keep him keen" or something to that effect. And, yes, this might work with some men—perhaps those with a masochistic side? However, most men don't want a woman who puts them or their friends down and never has a good thing to say about anyone. They don't want someone who constantly picks at them or makes their lives miserable. They don't like to be made to feel inferior and they certainly don't like to be yelled at.

All of this is completely and totally understandable.

But on the other side of this, do you really want a mousy woman who will sit in the corner and never say a word in her defense? Do you really want someone you can push around and do your bidding? Of course you don't. You want to be on equal playing ground with whatever woman you choose to date or even marry. In other words, you want to respect her.

Sure, you don't want a woman who won't stand up for herself, but, on the other hand, you don't want one who screams about your socks or the toilet seat. Am I right? It seems that being in a situation like this is like being between a rock and a hard place.

The only way around this is compromise. Things can be balanced out. One way to do this is to view the bitch angle from a different viewpoint. You might need to know that women who are bitches and who put others down do so because they feel inferior, not superior as you might think. They think that by belittling others, they can put themselves on a higher level. They don't realize how much they alienate others and that's because deep-down, they're hurting. And, yes, they are. Someone or something has happened to these women to hurt them deeply. You might not ever realize this because they're probably hiding their feelings, maybe even from themselves.

But this woman isn't like every single woman out there. Just because a woman stands up for herself and doesn't take crap from others doesn't make her a bitch. These women can assert themselves without sounding harsh. However, if you, as the guy who might be on the receiving end of this, misunderstand it, you might be apt to put this one in the dreaded category of the bitch. And what a loss you'd have on your hands then.

This is why it's so important not to paint every woman you see with the same brush. *Not all women are bitches.* Sure, some women are mean, vile shrews. This doesn't make them evil; it just makes them look bad. However, some women are just plain bitches who assert themselves when necessary. Learning to distinguish between these two will be a major factor in your dating success.

So, it might be worth mentioning to overlook when you can and to stand up for yourself when necessary. All women aren't bitches but if you think they are, you are just cheating yourself out of a lot of good loving. Besides that, if a woman just happens to be mean to you, it might just be PMS. And God knows there's nothing right a man can do when a woman is in the throes of PMS. Best to get out of her way and let her cool off until she comes back to her senses.

THE GIRL WITH THE COMMITMENT ISSUES

Let's say you've met the perfect girl. She's everything you want. You are *in luv*, as they say. Good for you! However, things start to turn a little, shall we say...uneasy between the two of you. What happens once you've got that great girl and you're in love but she suddenly starts acting a little...? I don't know... Aloof. What happens when you can feel her pulling back some, not wanting to go out as much?

Well, it's entirely up to you what to do, but first off, you need to decide if this is a relationship you want to keep. If not, let her go. Big deal. If it is, however, a relationship you want to keep there is something you can do to get her interested in you once again. And all it entails is that you suddenly become unavailable.

What you may have on your hands is a girl with commitment issues. Maybe she's missing the single lifestyle and her friends. So what? You've heard that saying, "If you love someone, set them free…" Blah, blah, blah. And that's what you do. You set her free. But while she's out there being all free, you're out there, too. You become suddenly unavailable. And how do you do that? It's easy. Just start pulling away. Pull back some. Just a little to let her know that you're not there all the time anymore. Not so much to make her think you're getting disinterested, but enough to let her miss you. This lets her know she's not the only game in town. This lets her know you have a life, too.

This may be hard for you because you probably really like this chick. However, if you don't do something, you might end up losing her forever. If you're afraid she might think you don't like her, then you're at risk for becoming her doormat. And that is a position you never want to find yourself in with a woman. Never be her doormat! No matter how good looking she is or how good in bed she is. This will only lead to you losing self respect and a man without self respect is like a dog without a cold nose. Well, that might not be the best analogy, but you get my point.

Keep in mind that if she starts pulling away and you start chasing her, she might just break up with you. This means she wasn't falling in love anyway. But never chase her. If she wants to run away, give her your frequent flyer miles. So what? She's not the only woman in the world, man! Get over her and move on.

Know that if you spend all your free time with any woman, you are pretty much asking for trouble. You will kill even the best relationship. People need their space. People need time apart. If you're all over her all the time, she will start to think you're crowding her and it won't be long before the ball and chain starts to weigh heavy on her.

But if you pull back a little, she might start to think she's not been acting right. She might start missing you and all the fun you once had. She might see you for the good guy you are. If you "forget" to return her call a few times, she might think you're seeing someone else. This will make her very jealous and if it does, she should be back in your arms in no time.

So, all you have to do is don't return a call every once in a while, tell her occasionally that you can't go out because you have "other plans" and "forget" to meet her a time or two. And when she asks what happened? Just say, "Oh, no, did I do that? I must have got the dates mixed up or something. Sorry."

It all becomes about not being someone's bitch. It all becomes about being "unavailable" to someone else every waking minute of the day. Once you do this, once you let her know you can get on without her just fine, more than likely, she will straighten up. Once she sees that she's about to lose something great, she might just come back home. I mean, if she's already pulling back from you, what could it hurt for you to do the same? You're just beating her to the punch.

Now, keep in mind that this might backfire and she might just go ahead and pull the plug on the relationship. (*Remember that this is a risk that involves real consequences.*) If so, then she was going to do it anyway, no matter what you do. And if that happens, she was never going to make you happy in the first place. No big deal. Just set her free.

YOU SEXY THANG!

Everything in life is about attitude and I think that's what we've been discussing pretty much throughout this book. If you want to be the man women want, it all starts with you believing you can become that man. It's all about your attitude and how you use it to your advantage. However, if you waver on this even just a little, you won't be the man women want. You'll be the man women avoid.

You don't want that now, do you?

Obviously, women don't approach men as much as men approach women. We all know it's your "job" to do the approaching or send the signal. But what if you could have it both ways? What if you could approach a woman and even have them approach you? What if you could have your cake and eat it too?

I think you can.

The key factor to becoming the man women want, as I've been saying all along, is confidence, confidence, confidence! Women absolutely love a man who displays confidence. This lets them know that if he's confident in himself enough to approach them, he's got enough confidence not to let them get away. This means, he's got enough confidence to buy them a drink. This means he's got enough confidence to ask for their number and use it to call them later in the week.

When you exhibit confidence, this lets women know that you haven't let life bog you down. You're just out having fun and that's all. This also lets them know you don't have any issues that might cramp their style if and when they decide to get together with you. Women, like most everyone else, don't like to be around a guy with too many issues. If you've got too many issues, it might be best to take care of them before you figuratively take it out on the dance floor. But if you come to meet them with a clean slate, all the better. More fun for all!

We've already discussed how you can be more confident in earlier chapters. But I will reiterate that you have to get it into your mind that you are worth it. You are worth some chick taking a chance on. You are worth a girl taking the time to chat it up with you. You're just worth it.

Keep in mind that women like to keep men guessing. That's why they play all those head games with you. It's fun for them to see you squirm. Women think if they lay everything out on the table all at once, men will run for the door. Women are afraid of looking too needy and they certainly don't want to look desperate. This may be why some are a little off-putting at first. They want you to want them but they don't want you to know they're thinking that. It's called having "mystery." But men may take is as being "elusive."

Is it any wonder, then, that the dating game is so skewed? No, but you shouldn't let this stop you.

So, this brings us to our point. When you're out and about, it's good to carry a "just don't care" attitude. This will make you sexy to women. So, what you have to do is that whenever you see a chick you think is hot, throw her smile, but then go right back to doing whatever you were doing—shooting pool, talking with a friend, whatever. It's best not to be too eager, especially at first. This will spark her interest and you might be surprised when she finds an excuse to come up to you and start a conversation. You might fall out of your seat when it's her that sends you a drink.

It could happen, you know?

This is why I said earlier that you can have your cake and eat it, too, especially, if you are willing to hold back a little and not act too eager. You can approach women and you can have them approach you. It works both ways. So, whenever it does happen, just be yourself. Be your sexy, confident self. When she comes over, say "hello" and smile like you're glad she's taking the time. When you go over to her, smile and say "hello" and know that she's going to be glad you took the time. And that's the key—take your time! Ease yourself into it. Don't think that just because you're in front of her you have to make a fool out of yourself. If you can't think of anything to say, just say, with a disarming smile, "This is kinda awkward, isn't it?" And then watch her relax and maybe even smile. Because it can be awkward. Meeting anyone for the first time *is* awkward. But do your best to keep it light and fun. If she knows how fun you can be, she will want to hang out with you more.

So, if you can act like you just don't care, you will pretty much become unstoppable. And you know why? Because you don't care! Your life isn't dependent on one date from one girl. And that means, you will begin to open yourself up to more possibilities than you ever imagined.

Funny how that works.

WHAT HAPPENS NOW?

Let's say you've met a great girl at a dinner, bar, club or whatever. You're into her and, as far as you can tell, she's into you. However, after a while, the conversation begins to wane just a little. What to do? It's simple. Just excuse yourself. If she asks where you're going, just say you need to make a call or something.

Taking a break will allow you to think of things to talk about and to relax a bit and get a little perspective on how you want to proceed. Now, this may seem like a bummer, but if you go back in and she's with someone else, don't freak out. Let her go and this will allow another to take her place. Never get hung up on one girl. *Never!* If the first sees that you've moved on, she's going to want back in the picture. And it will be up to you to make that decision.

Don't forget that you can get what you want. You just can't make someone like you. No matter how hard you try, you can never, ever *make* someone want you. But you can let them know that they've missed out on something. And when they feel like that, they will usually want to come back over to you to see what's up. This is why it's important not to get hung up on just one girl. When one sees that you can live without her, then she will see the value in you.

Like I have said, by being willing to let one go, you are allowing another to take her place. It's that simple. And once you do that, she might just want to be your number one. She might just see she was about to lose something great. And women hate to lose a man to another woman, just let me tell you. Even if she's not that interested in you to begin with, she will hate it when another woman makes time for you. That's a big secret not many guys know. I tell you this to enlighten you and, also, so you can use it to your advantage, but not to her detriment. So, use with caution.

Also, by being willing to walk away from her, you are presenting her with a challenge. She might think she's the one who can't think of anything to say. Remember that women can be shy and tongue-tied too. Men don't have the market covered on this, that's for sure. Keep in mind that no one likes rejection of any sort, so if she sees she's about to "lose" you, she might perk up or she might just be honest and say, "I'm sorry, I'm not good at meeting new people." And this can happen to the best of us. We get all hyped up to meet new people but when presented with one, we suddenly turn shy. Keep that in mind when you're meeting women and it might help you to relax a little bit more.

Remember, you don't have to settle on the first girl you meet and talk to. There may be things about this girl you're not comfortable with and, if so, be willing to let go and move on. This is where not being desperate will come in handy. If you know you can get another girl—and you can—then there's no reason to proceed with one who drives you crazy, and not with lust either.

IF YOU THINK YOU'RE COMING ON TOO STRONG...

I know it can be hard once you meet someone you'd like to get to know better not to come on too strong. You might have a fear that if she doesn't know you're alive, she could get away for good and you'll never see her again. This is why it's so important to be self-aware enough to know when you're about to do something foolish.

When you go out, just remember to keep it light. If you feel yourself starting to become too aggressive or get too hung-up on one particular girl, cool off for a bit. This is just insecurity guiding you to make foolish decisions. So, take a breather, get a drink, go outside, do whatever you have to do in order not to come on too strong. Just relax. You don't have to be in charge right now. You can let go of control. It's okay. It won't be the end of the world if this one gets away.

Remember the less you seem to care, the more women will want you. And the more you seem to care? The more they will want to get away from you. It's kind of like reverse psychology. This isn't to say, of course, that once you start dating that you can't show you care. No, no, no. It just means you don't have to show you care until you've actually got some sign she's interested in you. And you will know the signs she's interested. And what are they?

The signs she's diggin' ya:
- She smiles at you.
- She asks you for the time.
- She asks what you're drinking and points at it.
- She compliments your clothing, watch, shoes, etc.
- She says hello out of the blue.
- She touches your arm.
- She throws her head back and laughs at a joke.
- She pats your leg.

These are just a few signs, but I think you get the gist. The point is, you will probably know when she's interested. It won't be too hard to see, unless you're just completely oblivious to any human interaction. And I'm guessing you're not.

GIRLS' NIGHT OUT

There's a lot of confusion about why women are out in clubs and at parties or whatever. Some guys think they just show up to find a bad boy or whatever. Some think they're just there to hang out with friends. But why do women really go out? It's got a whole lot less to do with women than you'd think.

Mostly a girls' night out is about meeting and talking to and sometimes going home with men. Like I said, it's not that much to do with other women. You have to keep in mind that when women are out and about at clubs, parties or whatever, they, too, are looking for potential mates. They're not just there to hang with their girlfriends. They can see those chicks anytime. But when they've taken the time to dress up and go out, it's usually because they've got men on their mind.

The point of this is this: Don't get intimidated when you see a group of women together. They're probably bored with each other and wish some man—any man!—would talk to them. Why not be that man? Why not approach the group with a disarming smile and ask, "What's up, ladies?" Then see what kind of reaction you get. If it's relieved smiles, you've just hit the jackpot. If it's rolled eyes and sighs, it might be a good idea to retreat. But remember, nothing ventured, nothing gained.

However, keep in mind that just because women do, indeed, go out with friends in order to meet men, they're not just there to get laid. They are more than likely looking for someone to date.

Sure, there are some women who are on the prowl, so to speak. These women might just be divorced or looking to cheat on their men, or whatever. I say, always use caution. If you hook up with someone who has a jealous ex, you might be in for a world of pain. I'd suggest always asking questions before going the extra mile with one of these chicks. Sure, you might get laid, but if it costs you an arm, literally, then it's not going to be worth it.

The point of all this is to let you know what while women in groups may put off the vibe they're just out "having a good time," more than likely, they won't mind changing their plans if the "right" man comes along. So, why not be that right man? The key is to always be open to whatever new possibility presents itself. That's the important thing.

HEY, GOOD LOOKING!

We all know that becoming the man women want entails being confident. That's a given. Finding that confidence will enable you to have the ability to get out there and find the woman of your dreams. And one way to build confidence is to look your best.

It's a given that women like men who look good. Women like men who look their best. And looking your best is nothing more than tweaking what you already have. It does not mean buying out the stores or running up a credit card bill, so don't worry. This isn't about how much you spend as much as spending wisely. And if you don't want to spend anything, then that's entirely up to you. However, if you can get over your hesitancy about getting dressed up, you will pave the way to attract more women.

And what does it matter? I know many of you think that a woman should love you for you. And she should. And she will—once she gets to know you. But you have to have something for her to latch onto and if you look your best, she will see that you care enough to put the effort in. And that means she will be attracted to you all the more.

If you are feeling any sort of resistance to this chapter, then feel free to skip it. If it's not that important to you to go the extra mile, then so be it. But I'd be willing to bet that while you don't think you should have to look nice, you sure want the women you meet to do so. Am I right? And if this is true, isn't that being just a little hypocritical? Just think of it this way: Are you going to be attracted to some chick in a gunny sack dress or to the hot babe in a form-fitting outfit? I think the answer is pretty obvious.

You have to understand that people are attracted to attractive people. That's just the way it works. This doesn't mean that you have to go out and have plastic surgery or anything. That is not that I am saying to do at all. It simply means that you take what you have now and you make it better. It is about looking your best. And, again, if you are feeling resistance on this, why not stop right now and ask yourself why you are so resistant? Is it because you fear change? Do you think that someone is trying to change you? We are all resistant to change in some form or another but if you are so resistant that you get stuck and can't move forward, it might be time to do a little soul searching.

If you want to be the man women want, you have to get yourself unstuck in your old ways and get out there and get to it. No one is going to do this for you. No one can wave a magic wand over you and give you what you want. Being the man women want does entail being attractive to the opposite sex.

I know some of you are probably thinking, "But it shouldn't matter!" No, it shouldn't, should it? It shouldn't matter how you dress or what you look like. All women should love you for you. And here's the kicker—they will! But you have to first be attractive to them in order for them to do so. If you can't take that little bit of truth here, then how are you going to take it from someone in real life? If it makes you that uncomfortable, then don't do it. But this book is for men who want to have better dating lives. It's for men who aren't so resistant to change that they would get upset if someone dared mentioned that they aren't absolutely perfect. If you are such a man, then read on. And if not, ask yourself why.

Ask yourself this: What is holding me back? What is the fear here? And what you might find is that you have some deep-seated insecurity. And that's okay! Many people do. Insecurity can make the best of us lose it from time to time. Insecurity is also a sneaky little bitch. She rears her head at any opportunity to make us feel unworthy and foolish. Isn't it time, though, to tell her to take a hike? If you can find the source of your insecurity, then you can overcome most anything. Find it, deal with it and move on.

And in the meanwhile, why not look your best? By putting in the effort, you are telling yourself that you are worth it, you deserve the best and you are open to change. And if you're not open, then nothing can help you. It is only by letting go of control that you can move forward.

Keep in mind that no one is trying to control you. And—newsflash—no one wants to, either! We all have our own problems to deal with and trying to control someone is a waste of time. Why would anyone extend the effort to control another? It's beyond my realm of comprehension. But what I do know is that if you're a guy who wants a girl, then you gotta do something about it. If you want to date and be wanted, you have to look your best. I understand this. And maybe you should, too.

So, if you're a guy who wants to be the man women want and you want to look your best, I'm going to tell you how. I am going to tell you how to look more attractive to women. And, as you read this, just take what you can use and leave the rest. Tweak it for your individual preferences. Make your own rules about how you dress, but use these guidelines. I know all this won't apply to every single one of you, so just take what you can use and forget the rest.

While you might want to conform to the standard average Joe look, never be afraid to stand out a little. This doesn't mean to overdo it with gold chains and Italian leather loafers. This means, dress age-appropriately and keep your style simple and up to date.

Here's a list of things to think about:
- How stylish are your clothes?
- Is your weight about where it should be for your body type and height?
- Do you have a scraggly beard or goatee?
- Do you dress too young—or even too old—for your age?
- Is your hair going crazy and in all directions?
- Are your nails trim and clean?

Really think about all this. Consider it. You want to be the best you can be so the women out there will look at you first and not some other jerk. More importantly, you don't want them to not overlook you. If you don't stand out a little by being one of the best dressed guys in the bar, then they'll keep looking until they find him. And that's one reason those guys always go home with the hottie—they look good! That's why women want them. It doesn't take Einstein to figure this one out. It does matter what you look like. It's a hard truth, but if you can accept it, then you can free up that space in your mind to do something about it so that you are not out of the game before you even get a foot in.

In essence: The better you look, the more likely you attract better women. And, no, we are not talking handsome actor looks, either. We are just talking about looking the best *you* can. Everyone has lots of good qualities. You simply build on those you have. You might be naturally charming or a good flirt. Maybe you can fix lots of stuff or know how to hook up stereos. Whatever you have, you build on it. And by taking the guessing game out of how you're dressed—by dressing well and appropriately—you give women the opportunity to get to know the real you.

Now looking good does not involve obsessing. This should be a simple, easy process. Don't make it hard, either. It doesn't take a rocket scientist to figure these things out. All you need is to clean up a little. Trim your beard and maybe get a haircut. Buy a nice, simple outfit and good shoes.

It is not hard to take what you've got and make it work for you. It all begins by looking in the mirror and seeing what you can improve on. If you become the best you can be, it will give you more confidence to get out there and meet women.

Here are the things you might want to consider improving on:

- Weight. Many people could stand to lose a few pounds. No big deal. If this is you, then just lose a few pounds. It doesn't take much and what works in reality isn't some crazy diet plan that entails you weighing your food or eating a pound of bacon. What works is cutting back on your calories and exercising. It's really simple and easy. Never starve yourself, just watch how much you eat and don't ever overeat. If you do that, you will lose weight. There's no way you can't. (Be sure to check with your doctor before beginning any weight loss program.)

- Hair. One of the first things a woman looks at is your hair. Is it messy in a cool guy way or just plain messy? If it's the latter, it's time to clean it up. Get a haircut. It's that simple. Men are lucky because they don't have to put too much time or effort into their hair. Just make sure it's neat and trim and looks good for the shape of your face. If you are unsure, go to a stylist and ask them to make suggestions on what you can do.

- Nails. Many men overlook the importance of nice, clean nails. Don't overlook this! Keep your nails clean, trim and buffed. You don't have to do anything else.

- Cologne. Never overdose on cologne. Just a touch is all you need.

- Clothes. Just buy things that are in style and of good quality. With men, and again, you're lucky this way, it's the quality of clothes that matter, not the quantity. So you can get away with just buying a few key pieces to amp up your current wardrobe. The main idea here is for your clothing to be age appropriate and current.

One more thing. Never go out of the house looking sloppy. You do realize that women are everywhere, even at the grocery store, right? So, it's important to look your best at all times. Looking your best will make others take notice of you. It's that simple.

That's about it. It wasn't too painful, was it? Keep in mind, that once you feel like you're worth it and get over your insecurity issues, you can be more confident in your approach to women and dating. And confidence is what we're after, people.

LISTEN TO YOURSELF!

Earlier, we covered insecurity issues, but I think it warrants going over again. If you have insecurity issues, they will, inevitably, taint everything you do.

So, how do you know if you have insecurity issues? Just listen to yourself. What is your inner dialogue? What do you say to yourself? When you look in the mirror, do you cringe and pick apart your faults—perceived or otherwise? Do you constantly put yourself down? Do you tell yourself you're not good looking enough or successful enough or can never lose weight? Do you get angry with others when they offer helpful criticism? Do you ever explode with rage over a perceived slight? If you answered yes to any of these questions, you may just have insecurity issues.

You need to understand that no one but you can "fix" this. One of the simplest and easiest fixes is to evaluate yourself and your life. Sure, you might not be at the top right now, but does that mean you're at the bottom? Probably not. So, evaluate yourself and then think of ways to improve on what you've got.

Another good way to overcome insecurity issues is to stop looking for others to complete you. This means, stop looking for a woman to swoop into your life and make everything okay. You have to know—and believe—that you are okay *as-is*. You don't need someone to complete you. Sure, it would be nice to have someone *complement* you, but that's entirely different than thinking there is a part of you that is missing and until you find this one woman you won't be whole. You are whole right now. There's nothing wrong with you.

And that's the thing to keep in mind. That's the biggie—really and truly knowing and understanding that there is nothing wrong with you. You weren't born with a chip missing or whatever. *You are okay.* Sure, we've been discussing ways to improve upon yourself, but that's entirely different school of thought than thinking there's something wrong with you. This should not be misconstrued, either. Knowing you are okay, with or without a hottie, is what you're after. But also knowing that if you improve on what you've already got, your chances have more than doubled of getting what you want.

Keep in mind that everyone can improve upon themselves, even those people we view as already being perfect. We are humans and humans are always evolving. It's when we get stuck into destructive thinking that we get tripped up. But if you have basic insecurity issues, you may just be afraid to change. Insecurity can be a tough emotion to deal with. It can trip you up and hold you back and even make you perceive things the wrong way. For instance, someone might compliment you on your jacket or whatever, but if you have insecurity issues, you might take it the wrong way and think they're making fun of you.

Do you get what I'm saying? There's nothing wrong with you, it's just your insecurity making you feel that way. And if you constantly feel insecure and not "as good" as anyone else, then there's no way you can become the man women want. You've got too many issues already! And because of this, even if a great girl offered you a chance to get to know her, you might find something wrong with it.

So, the only way out of this is to first recognize that you have insecurity issues. Secondly, you need to make a valiant effort to stop letting your insecurity guide your life. And, lastly, you should try to find ways to improve upon yourself so that the insecurity just eventually fades.

It's not that hard to do, either. It's mostly listening to what you say to yourself and then correcting yourself. If you say, "I am a big, fat slob of a human being," then you would simply turn it around and say instead, "I am big. But then again, I am trying to improve that. It takes time and I am taking the time to do it."

This is quite easy to do. But most importantly, start listening to yourself. Listen to what you say to yourself and once you can do that, just start overriding the negative with a positive. Soon enough, it will become second nature and your confidence will soar. And that's what we're after.

WATCH YOUR MOUTH

There are a few things you should never say to a woman upon meeting, on the first date or, well, ever. If you've ever witnessed another guy saying these things, I'm sure you've cringed. And if it's you who been doing this, it's time to stop. Now, these are just a few examples and the idea is to not say anything vulgar or too personal. Ready?

Here goes:
- How far do you go on a first date?
- Are those real?
- Do the curtains match the rug?

No, no and no. Don't even go there. Ever. Even if you're thinking it, it doesn't mean you have to say it. Learn how to edit yourself. Think about what you say before it comes out of your mouth, especially when you first meet someone.

If you say things like this to women, all it makes them want to do is punch you. I won't sugarcoat this. You have to realize that they are not going to get the joke. If you have to say things like this, just say them to your friends and have a good chuckle. But if you feel the need to do this, maybe there's another issue going on and that issue is probably a lack of respect for women.

Think about this: How can you charm her if she hates you? You can't. So, make it a policy to keep these sorts of thoughts *inside* your head and never allow them *out* of your mouth. Give women the respect they deserve. They are human beings, just like you. Their feelings do get hurt and when some guy smarmily asks if their breasts are real, they know they're being degraded.

On the other hand, I think many men who do this sort of thing have an even deeper issue at hand, other than having a lack of respect for women. I think they don't respect themselves. I think they go into a situation with most women thinking they're already dead in the water before they even open their mouths. It's almost like a defense mechanism. They think, "She's going to shoot me down anyway, so let me go ahead and throw out the first insult before she gets a chance."

And the sad thing about this is, she might not even be thinking along these lines! She *might* be interested in you before you say something awful like that to her. But once those words are out of your mouth, all bets are off. She's going to think of you as the guy who put her down.

The point is mutual respect. If you want respect, you have to give it. Always go into a new situation with an open mind. Always give a woman the respect she deserves. If you say things like this, you're letting fear of rejection control you. And we've already talked about that. Let the fear go and let it dissolve.

But mostly, respect yourself enough not to make a fool out of yourself. Respect yourself enough to know that it's never appropriate to throw mud in someone's face, figuratively speaking. If you keep doing things like this, you might just come across a woman who can and will tear you down. And you don't want that. What you want is to feel confident. So, never put yourself in a position where someone can get a cheap shot at you just because you left yourself open to it.

I mean, what's the fun in that? Why not stay home and play video games? You're out and about because you want to meet someone. Right? If you just came out to put someone down, then why not just stay home?

Let me ask you this: What sort of high do you get out of putting someone down? Do you really feel that badly about yourself that you have to put someone down in order to feel better about yourself? If so, then this is an issue you definitely need to reconcile. So, keep it in check when you want to throw out a remark like the ones listed. See how your body feels. Do you feel anxious? Do you feel like you're being put down in some way? Just listen to your thoughts and how your body feels. And then sort through those feelings. I'd be willing to bet it's nothing more than insecurity rearing its ugly little head. So, get your insecurity in check and get on with your night. And never, ever, let it keep you from trying to make a connection.

REJECTION IS A BITCH—GET OVER IT

If you can get over your fear of rejection, there will be no stopping you from becoming the man women want. Granted, rejection is hard. No one likes being rejected. But to get hung up on it only means that you are not seeing the forest for the trees. Rejection is part of dating. In fact, it's a sad truth of life. However, if you can get over it, you can start living the life you want.

Remember we talked about the feelings of not being *good enough*? When you think of yourself as lesser than others, then you put out this vibe that you are. People can and will pick up on this. And once this happens, you kind of get in this cycle of *being* rejected. Soon enough, it's everywhere you turn and it seems as though you can't escape it.

It's like this: Once you start *expecting* rejection, you fall into the trap of always *being* rejected. This is why confidence is so important. Getting over your fear of rejection will lead to a more confident you. And even if you do end up getting rejected, you won't let it trip you up.

If it were only that easy, right? The fear of being rejected stops many people dead in their tracks. They get so afraid of being rejected, they stop attempting to do anything. They think, "Well, why should I? They're just going to reject me anyway." They refuse to put themselves out there for fear of embarrassment. And that's the thing that makes rejection sting the most, isn't it? That embarrassment. That humiliation. These aren't easy emotions to contend with and this is why many people stop putting themselves out there. The fear of being humiliated is overpowering. Why bother with it at all?

So, we can ascertain that rejection is pretty much fear of embarrassment, right? Sure. It doesn't take a genius to figure that one out. And nobody likes that red-hot stinging feeling of being mortified. I don't like it. You don't like it. Nobody likes it.

Unfortunately, it's part of dating. Sorry to tell you this. Rejection is part of dating. But if you can get over your fear of it, you can start to date more often and date better than ever before. Think of all those guys who've already given up because some chick dismissed them ten or twenty or however many years ago. He's taken himself off the market. He's let this one incident take him completely off the market. And for what? Why? Because he can't stand the feelings that being rejected gave him.

Rejection is just par for the course in dating. It's just part of the process. If you can't handle rejection, firstly, ask yourself why and then, secondly, ask yourself if you should even be *trying* to date since you can't handle the feeling of being rejected.

And that's all it is, fellas, it's a feeling. It's not a particularly pleasant feeling, but it's just a feeling. It's when you get tripped up on this feeling that you start to lose confidence. The idea is to not let it trip you up.

On the other end of the spectrum is acceptance. Every human being craves and needs acceptance. It's a basic human need. We need to feel accepted. We want to be wanted. And once we feel some acceptance, our confidence begins to grow. And as this happens, we experience more freedom from these unpleasant feelings and can begin to expect better things out of life.

But, unfortunately, getting that acceptance we need can be hard. But you have to keep trying. There's no other way around it. You have to keep putting yourself out there, even if all you think you'll ever get is rejected. And if you keep doing this, more than likely, you will finally find someone who will accept you. And once that happens, guess what? Even more people will begin to accept you. And then, at long last, you will have that acceptance you've wanted.

Before all this can happen, why don't you just do yourself a big favor and accept yourself? Why not just embrace everything about yourself? Embrace all your flaws and all your quirks along with your positive attributes. If you can begin to be more accepting of yourself, you can pave the way for others to be more accepting of you.

The fear of rejection might have started somewhere in your childhood. Perhaps an adult—parent, teacher, etc.—wasn't so accepting of you. Once this happens, as you grow and age, your need for acceptance increases, sometimes so much that it's all you can think of. That fear of never being accepted for who you are can be very disempowering. This might have been what tripped you up. If so, reconcile it and get over it. These people who rejected you in your younger years probably didn't even know they were doing it. And if they did, they might have been in so much pain themselves, they couldn't do anything else but. This is where forgiveness and empathy comes into play. Once you can begin to forgive those who've wronged you, you can let go of these rejecting feelings that cause you so much pain.

While this is all well and good, how do you get over your fear of being rejected? You just do, that's how. You look back and see where it might have started and you reconcile and you forgive those who rejected you. It's easier said than done, I'll give you that, but if you can do this, you can set yourself free of these uneasy feeling. You can also open yourself up to better people who won't do you this way.

You can also start putting yourself out there more. Women can't want you if they don't know you exist. If you're not out there getting noticed, then you're not doing yourself any favors.

Most importantly, *don't let rejection stop you.* Keep on going! Yes, you should certainly stop for a moment and recognize your feelings. This will keep you from bottling them up where they can later bubble up and drive you nuts. Just recognize your feelings, whether it's humiliation, embarrassment or being let down. Take a moment and *feel* what you're feeling. Always recognize and then reconcile your emotions. Just don't get hung up on them. And then get back on track. This is one of the most important lessons in this book. It's to get on track and to stay on track until you become the man women want.

One good thing to keep in mind is that if a person really likes themselves, it's harder for them to feel rejected. This is because they're not trying so hard to get acceptance. They're not putting that out there, which can be perceived as being needy or desperate or whatever. They're just trying to make a connection, not trying to be totally accepted and wanted and needed by everyone they meet. Because they like themselves, they know that others will too.

People who like themselves see the situation for what it is. They understand that if they get rejected it just means they weren't compatible with that person or situation. They don't filter all this through the narrow viewpoint of being accepted or rejected.

In the end, just know that if you expect rejection, you will more than likely get rejection. And if you focus so much on it, it can become a reality. So, why not turn it around and instead of expecting rejection, start to expect acceptance? Just tell yourself, "I'm a good guy and I will be liked by most people I meet. Sure, some of them won't be that compatible with me, but so what? That doesn't make me a bad person or them a bad person. It just means we weren't compatible."

If you begin to believe this, it will happen. This is called having self-acceptance. It's the best way to build confidence. So, get over your fear of rejection, get out there and get to it. Soon enough, if you keep a good attitude and get over your issues with this subject, you will find the acceptance you desire.

WHAT YOU'VE GOT

Whenever I see someone who is unhappy, alone and frustrated, I wonder if the main reason why is because they're not embracing what they have. By this I mean, don't they like anything about their lives, themselves or the people they know? Why are they so miserable?

If you refuse to embrace your life as it stands right now, it could potentially block newer, better things from appearing. I know this might sound metaphysical or whatever, but I think it's true. This is why I think *it's always a good idea to embrace your life as it is right now.* If you never appreciate what you have, you'll never be happy with anything you've got because it will never be good enough for you.

Take for instance the guy who always gets a new girl. Well, the old one looked pretty good, didn't she? And now he's going on to another one? And, soon enough, there might be another one waiting in the wings. What was wrong with the first girl? Probably absolutely nothing. He probably really liked her, but then another one just appeared from out of nowhere and she wanted to join his party. So he, basically, hopped from one bed to the next.

Now, I don't condone going from one girl to the next like this. Bed-hopping is not my forte. But I have seen it happen. And it always seems to happen to the same kind of guys, too. Who are these guys? They're not *that* great. But they are attracting women into their lives. How? I'd be willing to say that by appreciating the fact they have so many women into them, they open themselves up to having even more women. Mostly, these guys are just having a good time and that's what they've got going for them. So, they're attracting more good times into their lives.

Oddly enough, I've noticed that this kind of stuff never happens to guys who are miserable. It never happens for the ones who are desperate for it to happen. It's always the guys who already have it. Those guys always seem to have all the luck.

Or do they?

Seriously, are they really that lucky? They're just normal guys, right? But why are they having all the luck? Why do women love them? I'd be willing to bet that it has a lot to do with the way they embrace their lives. And who wouldn't embrace a life like that? Cute girls abound! Or, more specifically, cute girls who like to hang with guys like this abound.

The point is, if you don't embrace what you have now, your inability and, perhaps, refusal, to embrace what you have might be keeping the hotties at bay.

Take a moment to digest that.

You might be thinking, "But all I've got is junk!" Wrong attitude, my friend. Sure, what you have might be, in fact, junk. So what? It's what you have! And, most importantly, it's *your* junk. Until you recognize all the good things in your life and start showing gratitude for them, better things might not come along. If you can begin to appreciate what you have—even if you think it's junk—new things can start showing up. This allows more good things to come into your life. The gist is: Stop thinking that all you have isn't good enough. Once you do this and start seeing the good in what you have, you begin to embrace it. If you disown it, new things don't come as easy.

Mostly, you embrace what you have now because it's good. Sure, it might not be as good as so-and-so's, but it *is* good. Your car might not be a sporty coupe, but it runs, right? It does run, right? If so, that's good! You have a car that runs! Good for you! Now appreciate it for all it's worth, even if it has rust holes and the seat's broken.

This is called showing gratitude. And once you're grateful for what you have, you can have even more.

I understand that it can be hard. You might hate your job and, well, who doesn't? You probably can't stand the fact that your good friend, what's-his-name, gets dates all the time and you're alone every Saturday night. Understandable. But does what's-his-name have a mom that bakes delicious cookies? Does what-his-name even know how to change the oil in his car? Probably not. These are your good things. By embracing them, you are saying, "I'm okay. I am not in need." And this opens you up to more good things.

Now these are just examples. I know not everyone has a mom who bakes the most delicious cookies or whatever. The point is to find the good things in your life and appreciate them.

I know that if you have had a bad dating streak, it can be difficult, at best, to see the good in that. But this is just a form of resistance. You are resisting what you have and this just puts up a wall between yourself and what you want.

When this happens, you can get into a funk and I'm not talking about the George Clinton kind of funk. I'm talking about the doldrums. I'm talking about the funk that can last years and weigh you down. When this happens, you begin to wonder why everything is so hard and why you can't get dates and why you can't be happy. Then you start to procrastinate. And, in a way, you just give up. You, then, put yourself into a position where you can't change.

Well, get over it, man! This mindset is exactly what is keeping you from getting better. It's what's keeping you from being the man women want! But by showing appreciation for what you have and for how far you've come, you can get out of the funk! You do not have to wait until the perfect situation comes about to change. You can change right now, today, and start living a better life. If you only see the bad and never look for any good, all you are focusing on is what's wrong with your life. How about this? How about starting to focusing on what's *right?* Do that today. Find one good thing your life and focus on it. Love it. Hug it, figuratively speaking. Or, better yet, hug yourself. I mean, if you want to.

If you want to get from A to B, you have to make changes and one of the easiest changes is to start liking—if not loving—what you have, yourself included. Remember, you have you. And that's a start. Once you can begin to appreciate yourself, then you can begin to appreciate all you have and then you can start over.

It is never too late to change. Ever! If you could start today, in a year you could have your whole life turned around. But—here's the kicker—*you have to start.* You can't wait forever to turn it around because the future is today. You don't have to wait on something better, either. If you do this, you can get stuck waiting forever. And then your life can start to really suck as you wait on this "something better" to materialize. And all this starts happening because you don't appreciate what you have now.

So start appreciating it. That's all you have to do. This doesn't mean you're settling for less, because you're not settling. Don't get it confused because this fear of settling can and will block better things from coming into your life. All you're doing is showing appreciation. And once you start appreciating what you have, you can appreciate what you *will* have.

Being content does not mean becoming stagnant. It doesn't mean you're going to stay stuck. Just love what you have while you wait for the better things. If you really and truly want to move forward, you just have to appreciate what you have now. This is called not taking what you have for granted. This is showing gratitude.

And that never hurts anything or anyone. So why not try it? Hug it out and then wait for the magic to start happening. What do you have to lose?

FOR BETTER OR FOR LACK

One reason why you don't embrace everything about yourself is that you might be coming from position of lack. You might be fixated on what you "don't" have and never stop to appreciate what you do. When you are coming from a position of lack, you give up on things, sometimes even before they get started. But if you can remain positive, you open yourself up to things happening.

Once you start coming from a position of lack, lack is pretty much all you're going to have to look forward to. Lack can overtake your life and then you can start to feel like you're not good enough for anything.

And how do you get to this point? To the point of lacking? It's because it's what *you're feeling*. If you think you don't deserve anything in life, you won't be able to get it. Feeling like you deserve better means you *believing* you deserve better. For example, if you've never had a good, steady girlfriend before now, you're probably thinking that won't ever happen. It's like just because you've never *had* one, you will never *have* one.

Get what I'm saying?

I believe that what you think is what you manifest in your life. If you don't think you deserve any better, you won't get it. Ever. I've seen this happen many times. If you think that all the good women are taken, then so they will be. This is sort of like putting blinders on yourself and refusing to take them off. It's like you've got a notion stuck in your head and nothing can change it. This is coming from a position of lack.

If you've ever said, "It's not fair!" then you are definitely feeling this vibe of lack. However, if you actually believe you can and will find someone special—or several someone specials—then you will. This is called adjusting your attitude.

Attitude is everything in dating. It is everything when meeting someone new. It is everything about everything. If you have a bad, lacking attitude, you'll probably never get a better job, place to live or girlfriend. But if you can somehow stay positive and never give up, you will. It's all in your attitude.

The most important thing to remember is that when you come from a position of lack—whenever you say "It's not fair!"—you are basically putting yourself in a position to do without. However, if you can change your attitude, adjust your perspective, then you can change your life. I've seen it happen! All you have to do is recognize that you're doing this and you can and will set yourself up for a better future.

What I want to stress most in this book is that having confidence and good self-esteem is of the utmost importance. When you tackle issues like this and put them to bed, you are overcoming the very obstacles that have kept you out of the game for so long. And, if you're in the game, overcoming these obstacles will give you a head start. You are setting yourself up for better dating and, more importantly, a better life. And isn't that what you really want?

NOW WHAT?

Now that you've got it going on, it's time to actually meet some women and put all this into practice. It's time to implement what you've learned. You've taken care of your issues, your self-esteem is growing and you're more confident than ever. You might have even gotten some new clothes and waxed your car. And now it's time to spread your wings and fly. But, er… What's next?

Don't get stuck here, man.

I know that going out there and meeting women might still make you feel a little uneasy. And that's okay. It just means that you have to *feel what you feel*. Feel the feelings as they arise, whether they are fear, hesitation or whatever. And then go through with whatever you were going to do despite those trepidations. You have to push yourself out there. Take a big step and get moving.

And now the question is: But where do you meet women? If you are to put all this into practice, how can you do that? Where are all the women?

Get a clue. You know where all the women are. And you know where to meet them. And where is that? You meet then everywhere! After all, they do share the planet with you, don't they?

Keep in mind that where you meet them, exactly, is irrelevant. You can meet someone in line at the grocery store or at a rodeo or wherever. The important thing to remember is that it's not so much where you meet them than that you do meet them.

Sure, you can make a plan of action to meet women. This list will be comprised of your personal favorite places. Wherever you go, you are bound to run into someone. It's that simple. However, like I said, you can meet women just about anywhere. If you prefer to start dating online, then go for it. If you want to go to clubs, why not?

The point is that it doesn't matter what you do in order to meet women, as long as you do. There's no reason to make a list of all the places you can find women at as women are pretty much everywhere you are. The idea is to get out there and see who's available. And, because you're ready for this and you are putting out a good, positive vibe, women will start looking at you differently. And, maybe, they might come up and start introducing themselves. How cool would that be? It can happen, but you have to get out there in order for it to.

In the end, if you are still unsure of how to meet women, there are people called matchmakers. What these people do is talk with you, make a list of your attributes and then match you up with someone who will be compatible with you. Matchmakers, for some reason, are always overlooked these days. However, they can be a great asset in meeting women. The introduction is pretty much done for you! All you have to do is show up. And when you do show up, put your best foot forward and give this girl a chance. You never know why might happen.

WHAT IT ALL BOILS DOWN TO IN THE END...

I understand that this is a lot of stuff to consume. I know that I've hit upon a lot of hotspots but that's the point of the book. Just take the advice in increments and use what you can but be willing to be open to the rest. Hey, if it can help you land a hot chick, then all the better. Do whatever it takes to get out there and find yourself a good woman—or women. Your choice.

Always know that you weren't born deficient. What you might have lost over time is the confidence you need in order to date better. You have everything you need; all you have to do is wake it up and use it.

But what it all boils down to in the end is that it's all up to you. It's up to you to use the advice and it's up to your to go out and find women. It's up to you to overcome your issues and get some self-esteem. It's up to you to decide when you are going to take action. I want this book to inspire you to just do that. I want it to help you get over your fear of rejection or whatever else might be holding you back.

Regardless of the games people play in dating or the places they meet, the bottom line is about having relationships. It is not about one set route to the finish line. It is about *you* finding *your* path. It doesn't matter how you get there, it just matters that you do.

Keep in mind that there are plenty of single women in the world. And, yes, they're waiting to meet someone, just like you are. All you have to do is have the desire to meet someone and then see if it happens. Don't ever sell yourself short. If you are really and truly a good guy, it will come out and women will see it. Don't discount yourself and certainly don't discount them. Take the fear out of dating and watch what can happen. Your life could be totally transformed if you can put this into action.

And isn't that what you want? Total transformation? Lots of hot babes? A date on Saturday night? Someone to call when you're feeling lonely? If so, you can make it happen and it starts to happen when you decide it's possible. And it is possible.

Good luck. Have fun. Be safe. And, please, don't use any cheesy pickup lines. Trust me on that one.

Breinigsville, PA USA
25 March 2010
234944BV00001B/5/P